The Clutch Golfer Formula

How to Hit Exactly the Shot You Want Precisely When You Need It

by

Eric Jones, PGA, MA

and

Dr. Glen Albaugh, PhD

Published by Birdie Press
21 C Orinda Way #236
Orinda, CA 94563
www.birdiepress.com

This book is available in quantity at special discounts for your group or organization. For further information please contact books@iGolfU.com.

Cover design by Brian Johnson

Cover photo courtesy of Jeff Brehaut

Editorial consultant: Vic Williams

Special thanks to the athletes, coaches and golf luminaries who contributed their valuable time and knowledge for the Clutch Interviews. Every chapter leads with one of their stories: Jeff Brehaut, Pete Carroll, Bobby Clampett, John Dunning, Juli Inkster, Brandt Jobe, Scott McCarron, Nancy McDaniel, Michael Murphy, Conrad Ray, Kevin Sutherland, Kirk Triplett, Charlie Wi, Jeff Wilson

https://igolfu.com/course/clutch-golfer-formula-podcast-interviews

Clutch Test questions by Sports & Leisure Research Group

https://igolfu.com/clutchtest

ISBN-13: 978-0-9844171-3-1

Contents

SECTION 1: CLUTCH

Chapter 1: Why We Love Clutch

Triplett Wins!

In the 2000 Nissan Open at Riviera Country Club, Kirk Triplett stood on the 18th green poised to win his first PGA Tour event. Although Triplett held a two-stroke lead over Jesper Parnevik, both faced pivotal putts. Parnevik's 30-footer was for birdie, while Triplett had a tricky 4-footer for par.

Triplett knew that if Parnevik somehow made his birdie putt, Kirk's slippery downhiller would instantly become the most important putt of his life. Kirk recalled the way he had to shift his thinking:

> *"I thought to myself just before Jesper putted, 'Hey, you have to be prepared to make your putt. Accept this challenge. Be prepared to make the putt.' "*

In front of thousands of spectators surrounding the green, Parnevik's putt snaked up the hill and found the bottom of the cup. But even as the crowd roared and tension mounted, Triplett was ready. Using skills honed over many years playing on the PGA Tour and practicing for key moments precisely like this one, his formula for success was simple:

> *"I was totally focused on my routine, stayed in the present, took a deep breath, and let my stroke go automatically."*

He hit the cup dead center.

Clutch.

The Rest of the Story

But there's more to the story than Kirk just getting his first victory. Prior to the Nissan Open, Triplett held an unenviable record: the longest streak of starts on the PGA Tour without a win. It took him 266 tournaments, over 10 long years.

It's not hard to understand the internal pressure Triplett felt every time he got into contention, not to mention all the external pressure from the media and fans. Was this the tournament when Triplett would finally break through and the streak would end? The longer the streak went on, the more pressure there was.

It's easy to imagine how awesome Kirk felt when he sank the winning putt.

In his 267th tournament, Kirk Triplett finally captured his first PGA Tour victory. Triplett went on to win 10 more times, amassing career earnings in excess of $22 million. But that first win – and that key putt – was special.

We interviewed Kirk to get his thoughts on what it takes to be successful in pressure situations. You can listen to him describe that special moment in his own words. His interview is part of our extraordinary collection of conversations that make up the Clutch Interviews – a free bonus available online to all *Clutch Golfer Formula* book owners.

The Clutch Interviews feature incredibly valuable insights from stars of the PGA, LPGA, and Champions Tours, plus sports legends like Seahawks Coach Pete Carroll and *Golf In The Kingdom* author Michael Murphy. All of the interviews – including Kirk's – will help you play smarter and be a better, more consistent golfer. The interviews can be accessed at iGolfU.com.

Our goal is simple: we want you to experience that feeling of utterly triumphant exhilaration that comes when you hit exactly the shot you want precisely when you need it most. And we want you to do it often.

There's nothing else like it.

Why Clutch Is Captivating

We love riveting moments like Triplett's. We love the drama, the anticipation, the thrill of watching athletes bear down and come up big in the face of extraordinary challenges. Moments when the game is on the line captivate our imagination and put us on the edge of our seats. We love post-action breakdowns and dissecting what happened, why, and who carried the day. We love the excitement of game-changing moments, and we especially love it when *we* get a chance.

Every golfer we've interviewed can readily recall at least one – if not dozens – of critical situations and the shot they had to hit. When they pull it off (or don't), it can be the stuff of legend. Clutch shots earn us cheers or jeers, create fabled nicknames, and can even define an entire career. They are the warp and woof of our after-action tales at the 19th hole. Epic victory or epic fail, opportunities to seize the moment resonate with us forever.

Coming through when there is something on the line fills us with passion, energy, and the desire to come back and do it again. Regardless of age or skill level, golf gives each of us a chance to be the hero who came through when it mattered, hit the shot that won the tournament, took a few bucks off their buddies, or miraculously saved a round.

Athletes who consistently come through when they have to, particularly at the elite level, are the athletes we revere most. They have the uncanny ability to zero in and get it done in the biggest situations.

> *"Clutch is the most admired attribute in sports, the separator that differentiates our favorite athletes,"* writes Golf Digest's Jaime Diaz.

Of course we love being clutch. It's our shot at immortality.

Every Round Has A Pivotal Moment

Every round will present you with a critical moment. Think back to the last few times you were on the course. You'll nearly always recognize a particular situation or shot where your game could have gone either way. Maybe it was a drive. Perhaps an approach shot. Maybe a putt. It's always different. But there's always an inflection point that impacted your momentum. Big or small, those key moments define your round.

Every round will present you with the chance to be the hero. Learning to succeed in key situations isn't just an option; it is a must-have skill. It's what keeps your game from unraveling.

And it doesn't matter if you are a seasoned Tour player or a weekend warrior. It doesn't matter if it is a major championship or a two-dollar Nassau. No matter your level of play, if you got it done when you absolutely had to, you can say you were clutch.

Now that you know it's coming, are you prepared?

Are You A Clutch Player?

Anybody can hit a clutch shot. Once.

All it takes is a moment of focus and intent. Or luck.

Doing it consistently, though, requires a combination of skills. It takes a specific type of concentrated effort and willful determination. All effort becomes single-mindedly focused on a specific intent. There is no room for distractions or second-guessing. Making or missing the shot will determine the outcome. You have to get it right the first time. With so much at stake, the situation can seem overwhelming.

Performance skills are the key to tapping into the energy of crucial situations and using it to your advantage. They give you the ability to either:

1. Bring the moment down to a manageable level, or
2. Rise to the size of the occasion

Reducing the intensity of the moment is the common approach to dealing with pressure. Interpreting the situation as no different from any other normalizes it to something we are familiar with doing.

An alternative approach is to recognize the moment for all that it is and embrace it. Kirk Triplett rose to the occasion when he accepted the challenge at Riviera. It's like a clutch super-power. *Golf in the Kingdom* author Michael Murphy referred to it as "a*llowing yourself to be as big as the moment.*"

You're going to face critical moments. Our goal is to provide a roadmap to meet those moments, by detailing the skills to work on, different ways to structure practice sessions, and a routine to execute on the course. It's a way to find techniques that match your style, which is the path to a higher level of play and lower scores.

By using the Formula framework, you can design a routine that fits your unique style of play. With purposeful intention you can identify, develop, and excel at any performance skills you choose. And even though not every shot will be clutch, using the Formula consistently will elevate your overall performance and bring your game to an entirely new level.

Swing Technique Is Not Enough

You can develop the skills to perform under pressure, but it won't be through swing technique. Despite what the prevailing golf culture would have us believe, you can't develop performance skills through mechanics, and you can't buy a better game with equipment alone.

The average national handicap 50 years ago was 16.7, but today is only 16.3. Despite all the advances in equipment, golf balls, and technology, a half century of myopic focus on swing mechanics hasn't improved the index by more than half a stroke.

Everything can't be blamed on technique. But as the saying goes, if the only tool you have is a hammer ...

... everything looks like a nail.

We'd like to broaden the conversation beyond the swing.

The path to a higher level of play takes a different approach. It takes a new set of tools.

Change Instruction, Change Results

We don't mean to imply that technique instruction should be ignored. Solid fundamentals are the foundation of a great golf game. Fundamentals are the first skills to master when beginning to learn the game or when learning new skills. Better technique is a lifelong pursuit.

But in addition to technique, shooting lower scores requires *playing* skills. Golfers need to be taught course and game management, shot-making, and internal performance management techniques. And when there's pressure involved, golfers need additional skills in managing thoughts and emotions.

Blending technique instruction with playing skills, then combining them in purposeful practice, is the way to create a results-focused training environment that truly serves the golfer. We believe it is the sure path to lower scores. You will discover as many ways to improve performance from the inside as you will from the outside. Performance skills enable you to meet every novel situation with trust, confidence and resilience.

Our approach is a departure from the prevailing focus on quick tips, fault-fixing, and swing-based instruction. Far too many articles, analyses, and even teaching lessons focus on what is wrong with the golfer's swing and how to fix it. The swing may get fixed, but it doesn't necessarily mean results will improve.

That's why this is not your typical golf "fix it" book. It's not the way golfers typically try to improve. Not everybody will want to get off the "fix my mechanics" bandwagon.

But serious golfers will.

You don't even have to be a great golfer. Just serious about improving. We'll show you how to:

- Measure your performance
- Plan efficient training sessions
- Select the right drills
- Optimize your performance on the course

Plus you'll relate to the real-life examples from Tour players that will help you visualize and remember how to apply the skills when the stakes are truly high.

One of your most important tasks will be developing a repeatable pre-shot routine. That's why we created the action phrase "Lock, Load, Fire, and Hold" as the centerpiece of the Formula. Consistently executing your routine is the key to consistency on the course. The Formula is:

- A process that facilitates your ability to think clearly under pressure, enabling you to make smarter strategy decisions about shot selection and risk management
- A set-up routine that puts you in your most athletic position so you can take dead aim and make solid contact at impact
- A system to manage your thoughts and emotions, helping you to eliminate distractions and remain focused
- A step-by-step guide that will allow you to swing automatically and release freely with trust

Use the Formula to identify specific skills that will help your entire game. We've created a fill-in-the-blank template in the Resources section to serve as a guide to create your routine.

When identifying performance skills to include, pay particular attention to the way you react to pressure. Then structure your practice sessions to systematically develop your performance skills. Integrate them into your on-course routines in a way that enables you to effectively manage your thoughts and emotions.

One reason Tour players score better than amateurs is because they prepare better. Change your practice session to prepare like the pros. Include performance training and situational execution drills in every range session. Preparing correctly builds trust. It lays the foundation for confidence. When it's crunch time, proper preparation allows you to swing automatically, stay focused, and remain committed.

Being Clutch

Every golfer has the *ability* to be clutch. The secret to consistently hitting quality shots in key situations lies in developing your *skills,* and then using a consistent routine to *execute* those skills.

The *Clutch Golfer Formula* is your roadmap to better golf and lower scores. It will involve some experimentation as well as trial and error. There will be ups and downs. It's not always a smooth ride. It's not the traditional route to improving. What it does, though, is produce results. We are reminded of Frost's famous poem *The Road Not Taken*:

> *"Two roads diverged in a wood, and I –*
> *I took the one less traveled by,*
> *And that has made all the difference."*

We invite you to step off the swing technique bandwagon, take the road less traveled by, and see how it will make all the difference in the way you play the game. After all, the outcome is merely a reflection of the path taken to reach it.

Follow the guidelines in this book and you *will* make progress. You will hit more great golf shots, and your entire game will improve.

Coach's Advice

1. Every round will present you with a pivotal moment. Be prepared for it.
2. Use a routine consistently and practice it until it is automatic.
3. You're not going to win every time. Accept failure as an opportunity to learn, and resolve to keep trying.
4. Put in the work that is required to reach your dreams.
5. Clutch is fun! Believe in yourself.

Chapter 2: Defining Clutch

You're likely familiar with the phrase *"attitude is a choice."* So is adopting a clutch mindset. It is entirely within your control.

Greatness is independent of physical talent. As Juli Inkster's story points out, being a champion isn't about winning. It's about facing and overcoming challenges. The more conversant you are about the nature of pivotal situations, pressure, and the performance skills to manage yourself, the more successfully you'll stand up to those challenges.

As we discuss clutch situations, shots, players and performances below, keep in mind how your choices influence your success rate.

Juli Inkster: A Champion's Mindset

Juli Inkster knows how to thrive under pressure.

As an amateur she won three consecutive U.S. Women's Amateur titles, won the California State Amateur Championship, was California's 1981 Amateur of the Year and was named the 1982 Bay Area Athlete of the Year. She was a three-time All American at San Jose State, played on the winning U.S. Curtis Cup team, and was a member of the World Cup team in 1980 and 1982. As a professional she won 44 times on the LPGA Tour, including seven majors. She is not only a Hall-of-Famer, but also the unprecedented three-time captain of America's Solheim Cup team.

Juli Inkster is the epitome of mental toughness. She credits her success to her mindset:

> *"I was never the best ball striker. I was never the best putter. But I was a grinder. And I was a competitor. I didn't like to lose. There were plenty of times that I was down. But I never give up. That's really what made me good."*

Juli learned to embrace the moment.

For Juli, that translated into feeling excited to be in key situations. She looked forward to the chance to hit that pivotal shot. It also meant not worrying about the outcome and not fearing failure. Her focus remained centered on getting it done – sometimes through sheer willpower alone.

Although she knew she wouldn't always succeed, she never gave up. Juli remained steadfast in her belief that she could win the day. It is an attitude she's been cultivating since she started competing at age 15. She always wanted to be in the hunt down the stretch, and she used losses to light a fire under her motivation.

One of Juli's biggest challenges in coaching the Solheim Cup team was establishing a positive mindset in the face of incredible pressure. She recapped her message to the team in her Clutch Interview:

> *"In the Solheim Cup you're playing for your country. It's the biggest stage in women's golf and everybody's watching. But if you think that way you're going to fail."*

Practicing under pressure develops your ability to bounce back from mistakes. But sometimes it takes the push of a coach or mentor to get you back on track.

> *"Make it like any other day in an LPGA tournament. Just do what you do. Don't do anything else. Don't do anything more. I'm not asking anything else. All I'm asking is for you to give 100 percent and play free. Have fun. You're going to hit some bad shots. Don't make it like going to the dentist. Don't be afraid. Play free and have fun."*

A trusted coach can remind you of who you are and why you should believe in your abilities. That's what Juli did for Lexi Thompson during her singles match.

Lexi – arguably the best player on the 2017 team – got off to a slow start, going four down through the first four holes. Juli knew Lexi needed a pep talk. Advisory coach Jeff Brehaut described Juli's conversation to get Lexi back to who she was:

> *"Look, you're my best player. Let's go. You've made six birdies on the back side many times. Settle down. Do what you do. Go win a hole. One at a time. And the next thing you know, Lexi turned back into Lexi."*

Although it ended in a tie, the match turned into one of the best in Solheim Cup history.

As Juli said:

> *"We all know that golf is hard. Very hard. And if you're not your best friend out there, no one else is going to be. So be kind to yourself. Be positive. You're going to hit some bad shots. Everybody does. It's how you recover from those shots that makes you a champion."*

From her experience as an all-time player, Juli knew her mission was to coach the players to trust themselves and their game. She knew their ability to execute would emerge. Her team went on to win their second consecutive Solheim Cup by a score of 16-1/2 to 11-1/2.

As Inkster's example points out, clutch is a mindset that allows your skills to emerge. As a player, it was her mindset that helped her hit pivotal shots in challenging situations. As a coach she drew on her own experience to help younger players do the same thing: recognize and acknowledge the challenge, and then trust in their capabilities so they could remain focused on what they needed to do.

How Do We Define Clutch?

The journey begins with an understanding of what clutch really means. Our students are all athletes. They've all been in situations where they've had to hit important shots. Plus, we've all been well-trained as spectators by TV and radio broadcasters, who earn their keep by pointing out the implications and nuances of critical situations. It keeps the game exciting and the drama building.

Examining the many facets of performing under pressure allows us to break it down and gain valuable insights into the skills that contribute to success in key situations:

1. **Clutch Situations**
2. **Clutch Shots**
3. **Clutch Players**

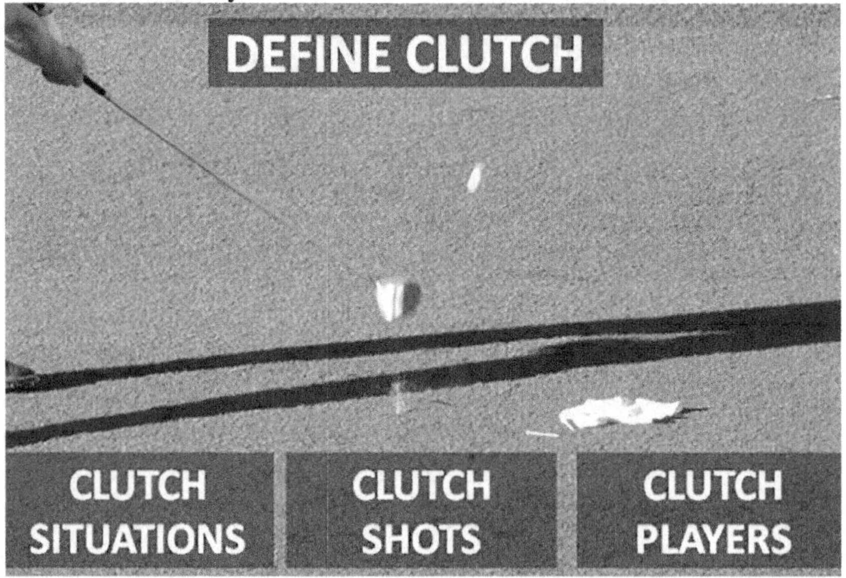

What Are Clutch Situations?

Take a moment and consider how you would define a clutch situation.

More than likely your definition will include words such as *pivotal, crucial, change in momentum, turning point, difference maker, outcome changer*, or similar descriptions. It's also likely to include qualifiers such as *determining the outcome, the difference between winning and losing*, or something similar.

As a golfer and an athlete you've already experienced many pivotal situations. But what makes these situations different from any other shot?

What About Pressure?

The common aspect of all clutch situations is pressure.

As athletes we naturally want to win. We are, after all, the hero of our own life narrative, and heroes carry the day. Opponents, on the other hand, are equally determined to have the outcome go *their* way. If somebody is going to win, someone *else* has to lose. Pressure builds when the outcome is in the balance and winning becomes paramount.

When we say it is a clutch situation, we acknowledge the added pressure that comes from the moment when the athlete *must* make a play. They *have* to hit a decisive shot if they want the outcome go their way. If they're one down in a match with one to go, they *have* to win the hole to turn the match around. Pressure, added to the imperative for immediate results, creates a clutch situation.

Most golf fans can readily name plenty of examples. In the 2017 British Open, Jordan Spieth bogeyed the 13th hole to give Matt Kuchar the lead with five holes to play. It was a pivotal moment for Spieth, who had been leading the tournament. Spieth *had* to do something if he wanted to win. He went birdie-eagle-birdie-birdie to shoot 5-under over the next four holes, ultimately winning by three shots.

Some of the most memorable pressure-packed situations involve a final-round charge or overcoming a major obstacle: Arnie's final round 65 in the 1960 U.S. Open to overtake Hogan and Nicklaus; the U.S. Ryder Cup team's come-from-behind victory in 1999; Johnny Miller's final round 63 at Oakmont to overcome a 6-shot deficit and win the 1973 US Open. Or the time you came roaring back on the last three holes to win the day with a superb up and down on 18.

But clutch doesn't always mean coming from behind. Nor does it mean hitting epic shots. Sometimes it is simply maintaining a lead. As former Green Bay Packers coach Mike McCarthy said,

> *"The ability to close a game when you are ahead is just as key as winning a game when you are behind."*

Even with the lead, you still need to execute. That's why developing the ability to execute *under pressure* is so important. You know you will face important situations. Your skill at managing your emotions, eliminating mental distractions, and committing to your strategy will determine the outcome. And you can become very skilled at managing the way you think, feel, and act. It is the key to responding well in any pressure situation. It is how you allow yourself to be as big as the moment.

What Are Clutch Shots?

Clutch shots are singular and defining. They are the one shot that turns the tide or seals the victory. They're game changers. They are the shot you need, when you need it most. They are at the pointy end of the spear: the moment when the pressure is most intense.

In the 2011 PGA Tour Championship, Bill Haas found his ball half-submerged in the water on the second playoff hole. At stake were the Championship, the FedEx Cup, and a $10 million prize.

> *"It was an all-or-nothing shot." said Haas. "If I don't pull it off I'm shaking Hunter's [Mahan] hand."*

With his right foot in the water, Haas blasted his pitch to three feet, made the putt, and went on to win it all on the next hole.

In the 2005 Masters, Tiger Woods holed out his pitch shot on the par-3 16th hole for birdie, even as the announcers were declaring par unlikely and bogey a probability.

Instead of losing the lead, Tiger went on to win his 4th green jacket, defeating Chris DiMarco in a playoff. Watching Tiger's ball trickle down the hill, hang on the lip, and then slowly topple into the cup is an enduring image of an outcome-changing shot.

In the 1982 U.S. Open, Tom Watson came to the 17th hole at Pebble Beach tied for the lead at 4-under with Jack Nicklaus. Watson's chip-in out of the thick fescue was iconic. With his caddie admonishing him to get it close, Watson said, "*I'm not trying to get it close. I'm going to make it.*"

Watson went on to defeat Nicklaus by two shots. To this day it is not uncommon to see golfers walk to the back of the 17th green and drop a ball to see if they can replicate Watson's shot. Few of them even make the green out of the heavy rough.

In the 1999 PGA Championship at Medinah, Sergio Garcia hit a big, slicing 6-iron from behind an oak tree on the 16th hole. Garcia's race across the fairway and leap into the air is another iconic image, showing how vividly clutch shots capture our complete attention.

Even Sergio could hardly wait to see if he'd pulled off the shot.

The list of game-changing golf shots is endless: Robert Gamez holing out on the 18th from 176 yards at Bay Hill (there's even a plaque on the spot in the fairway commemorating the shot); Corey Pavin's 4-wood to the 18th green at Shinnecock to win the U.S. Open; Larry Mize's "Mize Miracle" chip-in in a playoff to win the 1987 Masters.

Ben Hogan's 1-iron on the 18th at Merion in the 1950 US Open, captured by Hy Peskin, is arguably one of the most memorable golf images of all time.

These are examples of extraordinary clutch shots. We tend to remember them with greater clarity because they are such focused moments.

But clutch shots aren't always epic. Your most important shot of the day may be just getting that first drive in the fairway.

Most rounds, in fact, are characterized by a series of little moments that you don't realize were important except in hindsight. But taken together, as Brandt Jobe related: a close pitch there, an approach shot there, a key putt down the stretch – all the little get-it-done shots add up to a good score.

Even though your key shot won't end up on The Golf Channel, it will be important to *you*, and that's what matters. You are the one who has to get it done when the heat is on. Our goal is to show you how focus, intention, trust, and deliberate practice will enable you to pull off the shot you need, with consistency, regardless of the situation.

What Are Clutch Players?

Clutch players are the athletes who have a track record of getting it done. They consistently come through with shots they need, whether it is to come from behind, or maintain a lead until the end. They don't succeed every time, but they do with enough regularity that it *seems* like they do.

Hitting one great shot, though, doesn't make you a clutch player. Hitting them consistently does. Performing consistently under pressure is not the result of luck. It takes specific performance skills, which must be developed and practiced.

We encourage every golfer to set a long-term goal to turn themselves into a *clutch player*. Learn what it takes to be prepared to come through in challenging situations. Not only is it the most fun in golf when you do, but the benefits to your confidence, self-efficacy, and mindset are deep and long-lasting. Knowing that you are the kind of person who is dependable – especially in a tight spot – is a powerful mindset. And not just for golf.

What Are Clutch Performances?

Sometimes the overall performance rates as clutch.

We've all seen epic battles where the players make shot after shot, like heavyweight fighters trading devastating blows round after round. It's not just one shot that turns the tide. It is one tough situation after another, shot after shot, that makes a clutch performance.

Sergio's duel with Tiger in the 1999 PGA Championship was an example. Both players staged amazing performances. Sergio's 6-iron on the 16th, and his fairway leap, was a clutch shot as well as highly memorable. But Sergio didn't win the tournament. Tiger did.

Tiger's play that day was a clutch *performance.* He didn't hit a spectacular 6-iron from behind a tree. But Tiger did *what he had to do, when he had to do it.*

Tiger shot 11-under the first three rounds of the Championship. He shot even-par the final round. But it was what he needed to do. And as was evident by Tiger's exhaustion in the post-round interview, it took an amazing amount of focus, intensity, and mental toughness to pull it off.

Clutch performances take into account the entirety of the effort. Not just the final putt, but all the drives, chips, and approach shots that came before. Everything has to work right for a clutch performance, including strategic thinking and decision making: when to go for it and when to be patient.

Even then, like Sergio, you may not carry the day. Tour veterans have a saying: "*Sometimes you do, and sometimes you don't.*" What clutch players don't do is lose the belief that they can.

It takes sustained focus and intention. It is both exhausting and exhilarating, yet it should be the ultimate goal of every golfer. Your deepest satisfaction will come from maintaining a high level of play over an extended period of time. As psychologist Theodore Rubin said:

> *"Happiness does not come from doing easy work but from the afterglow of satisfaction that comes after the achievement of a difficult task that demanded our best."*

You may not win, even after turning in a clutch performance. But you *will* find that Rubin's "*afterglow of satisfaction*" plays a key role in maintaining your commitment to train with focus and intensity.

Closers: A Special Kind of Clutch

Then there are the special kinds of clutch players: the closers. In the last moments of the match, when everything hinges on a single shot, closers relish the opportunity to make the play that wins the day.

Closers are the ones who want the ball at the end of the game. Every baseball team has a closer. It's one of the most important roles on the squad. Pressure situations are the *only* moments they face.

The closer mentality develops from repeated exposure to last-minute, crucial situations. Instead of fearing do-or-die moments, closers learn to look forward to them. The extreme pressure of the situation is when they feel most alive. They *want* to be there. They *want* the chance to be the difference-maker.

Winning isn't the motivation: it's the thrill of being in the hunt. Like Juli Inkster, they love being in the thick of the competition when winning or losing hangs in the balance. They just want the chance to have their shot at the end of the round.

Billy Casper said in *The Big Three and Me:*

> *"The players who thrived didn't just execute the swing when it mattered; they relished the opportunity to be able to do so. They loved to compete. They loved being in the thick of it on the final few holes. They didn't shy away from pressure, they yearned for it."*

Eric Jones (author) won his first World Long Drive Championship title in 2003 with a clutch shot. He had to come from behind, hitting a 381-yard drive on his sixth and final shot, to win by a mere 29 inches. When he won his second title in 2012, nine years later, it was by coming from behind once again, and once again on his sixth and final ball, hitting a 369-yard drive to win by three yards.

Walter Hagen once said that a man is lucky to win the U.S. Open once, but if he wins it twice, it's not luck.

Eric entered every long drive competition with a closer's mentality. His goal was simply to get into position to have a chance to win, and then see what happened. Every competition was a learning experience. His first title in 2003 came from a clutch shot. When he won his second World Championship title in 2012, it was because he had learned how to thrive in pressure-packed situations.

Over a 12-year period competing in Long Drive, Eric was always in the thick of the competition. He recorded three Top-3 finishes, two Top-5s, and only once finished outside the top 10. Each year he came away with a better understanding of what worked best for him.

Two things contributed most to Eric's second championship title:

1. Experience. Knowing that he had already done it gave him the confidence to believe that he could do it again.
2. Preparation. He continued to refine his training program until he could stand on the tee with full confidence that he had done everything he could to be prepared for the moment.

He rehearsed under pressure situations so that when the moment came, there were no surprises. He was looking forward to it, and was always ready to compete at his highest level.

Scott McCarron provides another example. At the 2017 Dick's Open in Endicott, New Jersey, McCarron came to the final hole with a one-shot lead over his good friend Kevin Sutherland. McCarron's drive went wide right, ending up in the rough behind a wall of trees. When Sutherland knocked his second shot to eight feet, McCarron faced a critical situation. Sutherland was in great position to make birdie. McCarron needed not one but *two* big shots.

McCarron's shot from the rough rocketed over the trees and landed 15 feet below the cup. Walking up to the green, as he later told Dr. Glen, he "*was already seeing that putt go in.*" And it did, sealing championship with an eagle and a one-shot victory.

Locking in to the visual image of the putt going into the hole was a powerful way for Scott to maintain his focus. McCarron is very skilled at it because he diligently practices it during his practice and training sessions, using techniques Dr. Albaugh has been coaching since Scott first turned pro.

Closers like Scott McCarron develop a closer mentality. They rise to the size of any situation. They relish the opportunity. Their mindset, though, is always backed up with preparation. They believe they are up to the challenge in any situation.

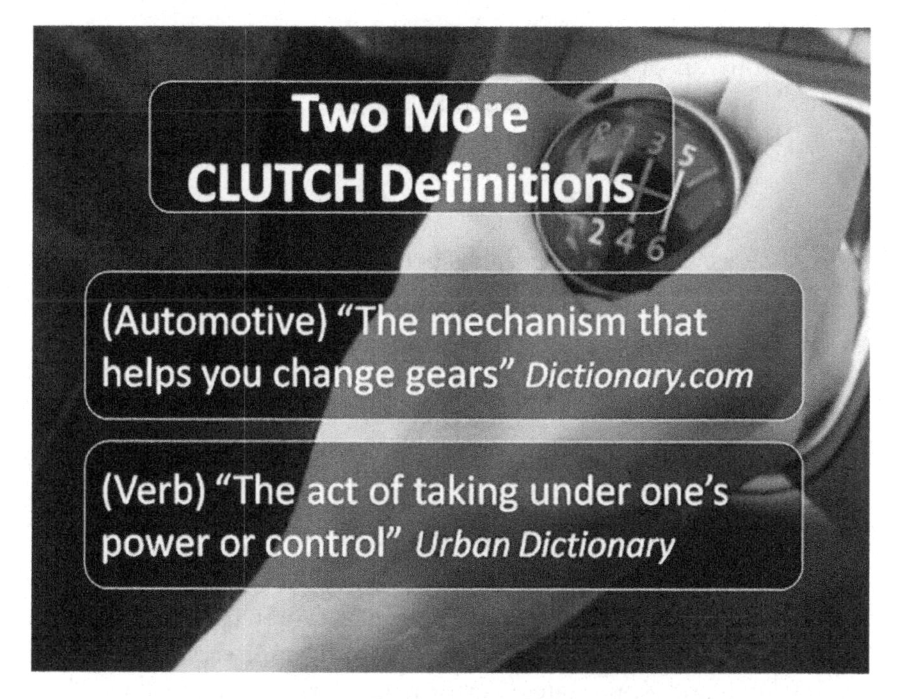

Clutch: Shift Gears and Take Control

Clutch can also mean:

1. A device to change gears
2. Grasping or seizing control

Automotive: The first definition is from the automotive world: a clutch is the mechanism that helps you change gears. To apply it to golf, think of clutch as a mechanism to change your level of play. You can purposely shift your focus and intention to a higher gear. You can also shift your body and mind to the center, where you will be more physically and mentally prepared to act.

Action Verb: A second way to think about clutch is the act of grasping or holding strongly to seize control. Think of it as a way to seize the moment in a challenging situation. To own it. Carpe diem. Take charge. Exert your will.

You can seize only what is within your control. You can't control the outcome. But you can control your focus, intention and belief. You can choose the way you think, feel, and react. You can purposely create response patterns that help you perform under pressure.

You can even choose a shot to be clutch. If you aren't having a great round, you can pick a shot and decide it's going to be the turning point. You can choose to change momentum, *any* time, on *any* shot. Your choices determine what kind of player you will be.

The Zone vs. Clutch

The Zone vs. Clutch: which one is better?

With the abundance of research in Sport Psychology on Flow States (a.k.a. the Zone), researchers were surprised to discover the number of similarities between them. A study by Swann et al. and published in the 2017 *Journal of Sport Psychology* found:

> *"Common to both states are the experiences of enjoyment, enhanced motivation, perceived control, altered perceptions of time and the environment, absorption, and confidence."*

Both states of play are desirable. Both are associated with peak performance experiences. A quiet mind, centered in the present moment and focused solely on the task at hand, is a precursor to both Clutch and Zone states. Performance coach Steve Yellin said:

> *"The key to athletic success is a quiet prefrontal cortex. And while that may sound complicated, it's not. We've all had the experience when our prefrontal cortex did not meddle in a stroke. At those times it felt like the perfect stroke happened all by itself, without our even thinking about it."*

However, there are also important differences between Clutch and the Zone.

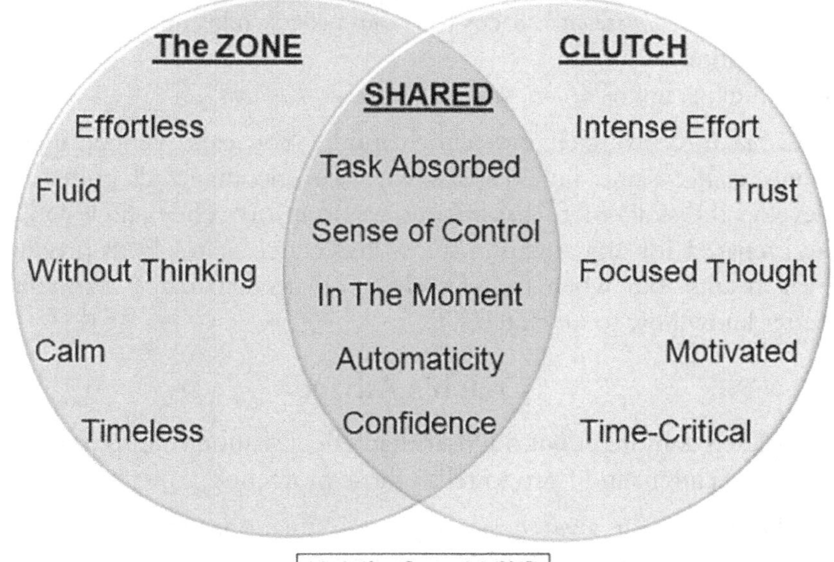

Adapted from Swann et al. (2017)

When we are in the zone we describe the experience using words like *effortless, timeless, easy, in-sync, fluid, in the moment*, and others. When we describe clutch experiences, we use different words such as *intense, focused, purposeful, do-or-die, and intentional.* The Swann et al. study also states:

> *"Clutch states differ from flow (the Zone) in a number of ways while sharing a range of overlapping characteristics. Specifically,*

- *Clutch states are characterized by complete and deliberate focus on the task; whereas flow is characterized by effortless attention.*
- *Clutch states involve heightened awareness of the situation and its demands; whereas flow involves positive feedback and feelings that 'everything is going to plan.'*
- *Clutch states involve intense effort, in contrast to flow, which is characterized by an effortless, automatic experience."*

The problem with relying on being in the Zone is that you can't predict when it's going to happen. You can't force yourself into the Zone. It seems to happen when it happens. Clutch states, on the other hand, can be reached with the right preparation and knowledge:

- Clutch is *making* things happen, while Flow is *letting* things happen
- Clutch is *heightened* situational awareness, whereas Flow is *passive* engagement
- Clutch is *intentional* focus on the task, while Flow is *effortless* attention
- Clutch is intense *effort*, whereas Flow is *fluid and easy*

You *can* force yourself into clutch mode. You can even be in the Zone at the same time! That's why we encourage all golfers to develop the skills of focus, intention, and effort. They allow you to be prepared for any situation. Flow and clutch states both produce peak results. But when facing a shot you need to make *now*, you'd better know how to be clutch.

Coach's Advice

1. Clutch is more about mindset than talent. Embrace opportunities to be clutch, and learn to relish those moments.
2. Develop your awareness of pivotal situations, and consciously bring your full focus and intention to them.
3. Deliberately improve those skills and techniques you use when playing your best.
4. Own the moment. Learn how to shift gears when the situation calls for it, so that instead of the situation controlling you, you control the situation.
5. Be happy when you experience being in the Zone. But when you're facing a clutch shot, be prepared to enter into a high state of deliberate focus and intense effort.

Chapter 3: Clutch Secrets

Sometimes you chase a dream your whole career before you finally get your shot. You don't get many chances at the big brass ring, so it pays to be ready when the big moment does arrive.

Tiger Woods' childhood goal was to win more Major Championships than anyone else. He may or may not top Nicklaus's record (18), but we do know that he has only a finite number of opportunities left to do it. There are only four majors per year. Multiply that by however many years remain in Tiger's career, and you know how many chances he'll have left.

Tiger has been preparing to beat Jack's record his entire life. It's one reason he performs so well in majors. He expects to be there. He's ready for it. He's prepared to win.

When you have a chance to achieve one of your big goals how are you going to handle it? Will you be ready? Have you prepared?

Opportunities to realize your big dreams are precious. There will be a pivotal moment, when the goal seems tantalizingly within reach, where it could go either way. The first secret to making things go *your* way in pivotal moments is preparation.

When Scott McCarron won the 2019 Champions Tour Schwab cup, he didn't do it with a spectacular shot. He did it the only way you can win a season-long title: with spectacular consistency. His brilliant season included three wins, 14 top-10 finishes, and by finishing in the top 25 in 21 of his 26 tournaments.

Capturing the Schwab Cup wasn't a sudden break through either. McCarron's achievement was the culmination of many years of diligent effort, with each accomplishment layering on and adding to the next. The most important may have been winning his first major two years earlier: the 2017 Senior Players Championship.

Scott McCarron's First Major

Winning a Major was one of Scott McCarron's big goals. For many professional golfers, winning a Major Championship can be the defining moment of their career. McCarron chased his dream for 26 years on the Tour before finally capturing his first Major: the 2017 Senior Players Championship.

McCarron started the final day of the Senior Players Championship at Caves Valley six shots behind leader Bernhard Langer. Langer had won each of the past three consecutive Players Championships, and was the most dominant player on the Champions Tour. McCarron knew he'd have to play at his highest level to catch Langer.

McCarron rose to the challenge. He birdied six of the first 10 holes on Sunday and played solid, steady golf the rest of the way in.

But as Scott came to the 17th hole he was fully aware that the circumstances had changed. He saw that he'd played himself into a position to win, and he recognized that the way he handled the challenging final two holes would be pivotal.

The 17th and 18th at Caves Valley were considered the two toughest holes on the course. The par-3 17th is a difficult 215-yard shot to a green guarded by water on the right and bunkers on the left. The 18th is a long par-4, with a narrow fairway protected by half a dozen bunkers on the left and a stream running up the entire right side. Wayward shots were sure to find trouble.

McCarron had both great situational awareness and great personal self-awareness. He knew the situation. He knew what he had to do. He also knew how to stay in the moment, and how to focus on hitting solid golf shots.

Scott relied on the routine he had meticulously developed and repeated in practice. He knew that if he would just follow his routine, he'd be in position to execute. His preparation gave him confidence. Scott certainly felt the pressure, but it wasn't enough to overwhelm the trust he'd built through quality practice.

McCarron hit a beautiful 5-iron to the middle of the green on the par-3 17th and narrowly missed making birdie. He then followed up with a solid drive on the 18th, and an equally solid approach shot that gave him an easy par. He escaped the final difficult two holes to finish with a bogey-free final round of 66.

Scott watched as Brandt Jobe's final-round charge stalled with a bogey from the bunker on the treacherous 17th. Then the 17th claimed another victim, as Bernhard Langer's tee shot found the water. Langer walked away with double-bogey, and McCarron weathered the storm. McCarron finished with a 1-shot advantage over both Langer and Jobe to claim the championship. (Jobe was McCarron's roommate in college!).

McCarron was the only player to card rounds in the 60s all four days, and the six strokes he made up matched the tournament record for the largest come-from-behind victory in the Senior Players Championship.

Scott's play the final day was the product of his preparation. He played solid golf in a pivotal situation, and that enabled him to accomplish one of his life's dreams.

McCarron's Secret

The secret to McCarron's success wasn't his swing technique. It wasn't a miracle shot. The secret to his success was the many years of deliberate practice on the range leading up to that moment.

Scott practiced the right things the right way. He put himself under pressure in practice to develop situational awareness. He learned what he did best, so that he would know how to respond when the pivotal moment arrived. He refined his self-awareness through self-coaching. Then he stuck to what he knew.

In other words, the secret was in his preparation.

But not just any kind of preparation. It was smart preparation. It was deliberately practicing his playing skills – not just his swing skills – and systematically refining a bullet-proof routine that enabled him to execute under pressure. As legendary NFL Hall of Fame coach Bill Walsh said, "*If you're ever surprised in pressure situations, you're not prepared.*"

There was no surprise for Scott. Practicing his routine on the shots he knew he'd have to hit, and doing it under pressure, allowed him to execute on the course. He drew confidence from years of constantly testing his routine through competition, and that confidence gave him the trust he needed to swing freely without hesitation or reservation. He was confident he could hit the shots he needed because he'd already practiced them. His single-minded focus simply left no room for doubt when he faced a pivotal moment.

Some golfer burst onto the scene, achieving instant success. But they are rare. For the vast majority of golfers it is a slow and steady climb.

McCarron's success was a direct result of his preparation over many years. But as his example points out, consistently improving your execution through situational training, accompanied by a consistent pre-shot routine, are skills *every* golfer can master, regardless of the scores you shoot. By combining playing skills and execution training with your technique practice, you'll be amazed at how much enjoyment you'll have and how much more consistently you'll execute in novel situations.

Four Clutch Insights

1. **Clutch is a Playing Skill**
2. **Perform at Your Statistical Average**
3. **Follow a Consistent Process**
4. **Deliberately Develop Clutch Skills**

Clutch situations are opportunities for you to bring all your peak performance skills into play. Through studies, research, and personal experience, and interviews with players like McCarron, we discovered four insights about clutch and what it takes to be successful under the gun. These insights are a roadmap for your journey to better golf.

Insight 1: Clutch is a Playing Skill

If you are thinking about your technique during the shot, your focus is simply in the wrong place. Not one clutch golfer we've interviewed talked about their technique when they described how they hit their shots. They all described the imagery, the feel, the focus, or the mindset.

That's why every clutch superstar we interviewed religiously includes playing skills in their practice sessions. Playing skills, not technique, get it done. The great players practice shots under pressure first, so that they are prepared for them on the course.

Playing skills are about scoring. They are about shot-making and shaping the ball to a target on purpose. They are about controlling impact, trajectory, and ball flight. Playing skills enable adaptability: the ability to adjust to the unique lie, stance, and conditions and still make solid contact, because no two shots are ever the same.

Playing skills are also about organizing your thoughts, emotions, and behaviors to have a positive impact on your performance. They include following a process to manage yourself that automatically sets you up in the best position for success. Then they are about training in specific performance skills, in structured practice sessions, to transfer skills from practice to on-course play.

Playing skills start with a strategy, which includes an analysis and understanding what the lie, yardage, situation and conditions dictate for the shot. It includes knowing where to hit it, where not to miss it, and how to balance risk vs. reward. Then it also includes being realistic about what you can and cannot do, so that you can pick a shot that is within your capabilities.

Strategy gives you clarity. The more clearly you can picture the shot and the more comfortable you feel that it's a shot you can hit, the more strongly you'll commit to your strategy. Clarity also makes it easier to *remain* committed to the end of the swing.

Playing skills such as course navigation, game management, strategic thinking, pre-shot routines and a process for clear decision-making are the foundation for better scoring. And when there's pressure, it takes self-management skills to maintain intensity, focus, intention, and trust to hit the shot you want.

Focusing solely on your swing mechanics will not help you in clutch situations. In fact, having a technique focus while you are swinging is far more likely to make you do the opposite: choke.

Playing skills should be practiced just as much as swing mechanics. It becomes even more important to emphasize transfer skills the closer you get to a tournament or major competition. Playing skills prepare you for the unexpected.

Insight 2: Perform at Your Statistical Average

Being clutch does not require superhuman shots or extraordinary skill. It may come as a surprise, but clutch players don't do anything in clutch situations beyond what they are already capable of doing.

Remarkable as it sounds, recent studies of stats across all sports show that even the athletes we think of as clutch players actually perform near their statistical average in pressure situations. Whether it's basketball, football, baseball, or golf; whether it is LeBron James, Tom Brady, or Tiger Woods, the icons we think of as clutch don't do anything beyond their normal capabilities. It is the *situation* that makes the results seem bigger.

We've all seen golfers hit extraordinary shots in big time situations. But those golfers are *already capable* of hitting those shots. It may look like heroics, but it really isn't. Clutch athletes perform near their statistical average under pressure, and Tiger Woods is a perfect example.

Tiger's stats show he is clearly the best closer in golf history. When he had a 54-hole lead, he was successful in winning the tournament 54 of 58 times. That's an astonishing 93% close rate. Jack Nicklaus is second with a 70% close rate. After that, nobody else is in the same league.

But here's the kicker: Tiger's average score on his final round was actually worse than the average for his first three rounds: 69.4 compared to 69.1. In other words, he scored almost one third of a shot *higher* on his final round, and still managed to win.

How does performing at your average make you clutch?

One of the secrets to being clutch is to not change anything. When the moment is out of the ordinary, you'll feel like you need to hit an extraordinary shot. But you don't. Just do what you are capable of doing. as Jon Doyle said in *Baseball Training Secrets:*

> *"The first key is to NOT change a thing. Most hitters make the mistake of trying to do too much or something they simply cannot do. You hear the phrase 'Step Up,' but the reality is the players that 'step-up' simply do what they always do. They don't change a thing. And since pressure (internal or external) destroys most guys and makes them play at a lower level than they usually do, if you can just do the things you always do, you'll 'step up' without changing a thing!"*

Tiger knows how to win tournaments. His formula for success was to get in position the first three days, and then play to his average on the last day. All he needed to do was finish one shot lower than everybody else at the end of four days.

Once he was in position, all he had to do was what he normally did. His final round strategy was simple: hit to the middle of the fairway, hit it on the green, two-putt, and walk off with a 69. He knew that if he played to his average, the rest of the field would not likely catch up. And 93% of the time they never did.

Kobe Bryant and LeBron James are considered modern-era clutch basketball stars. Yet in clutch situations (when the score was within five points in the last five minutes of the game), their shooting percentage dropped compared to their historical average.

In clutch situations, Kobe's field goal percentage was 39.7% (2000-2012), compared to his career average of 44.7%. LeBron's clutch field goal percentage was 46.0% compared to his career average of 50.1%.

(spoiler alert: these players *scored* more in clutch situations, but they did it by taking more shots rather than by improving their performance).

In Tom Brady's record-setting 34-28 comeback win against the Falcons in Super Bowl LI, his pass-completion rate was 69.4% (43/62) – only slightly better than his season average of 66.5%.

What clutch players don't do under pressure is choke. They don't perform significantly worse than their average in clutch situations. Just performing at a statistical average is enough.

The truth is that most athletes *underperform* in the clutch. Including the pros.

For example, the win-rate for PGA Tour players who have the lead after 54 holes is only 40%. *Less than half!* Surprising as it may seem, even these highly accomplished athletes lose more often than not in the pivotal final round. Put a little pressure into the mix and suddenly everything changes.

The Shot Capability Zone

Clutch situations are not normal, so it is natural for the mind to think the shot should be beyond the norm. But that is not the case. Picking a strategy based on shots you know you can hit takes the stress out of executing the swing. The more normal and routine the shot, the better the chances for success.

We created the Shot Capability Zone as a way to picture the range of shots you *can* hit, relative to the shot you might *want* to hit. Shots within your capability zone will feel more comfortable and give you more confidence. Shots outside your capabilities have the potential to introduce interference from anxiety or indecision, leading to tension, uncertainty, second-guessing, over-control, and loss of focus.

Use it as a strategy tool to quickly evaluate your capabilities vs. the risks and skill levels. Consider all the risk/skill factors as you develop your strategy, but make a habit of choosing shots that are within your capabilities. The shot you choose may be at the very edge of your capabilities, but knowing it is a shot you can hit helps normalize it, and is an important step in managing pressure situations.

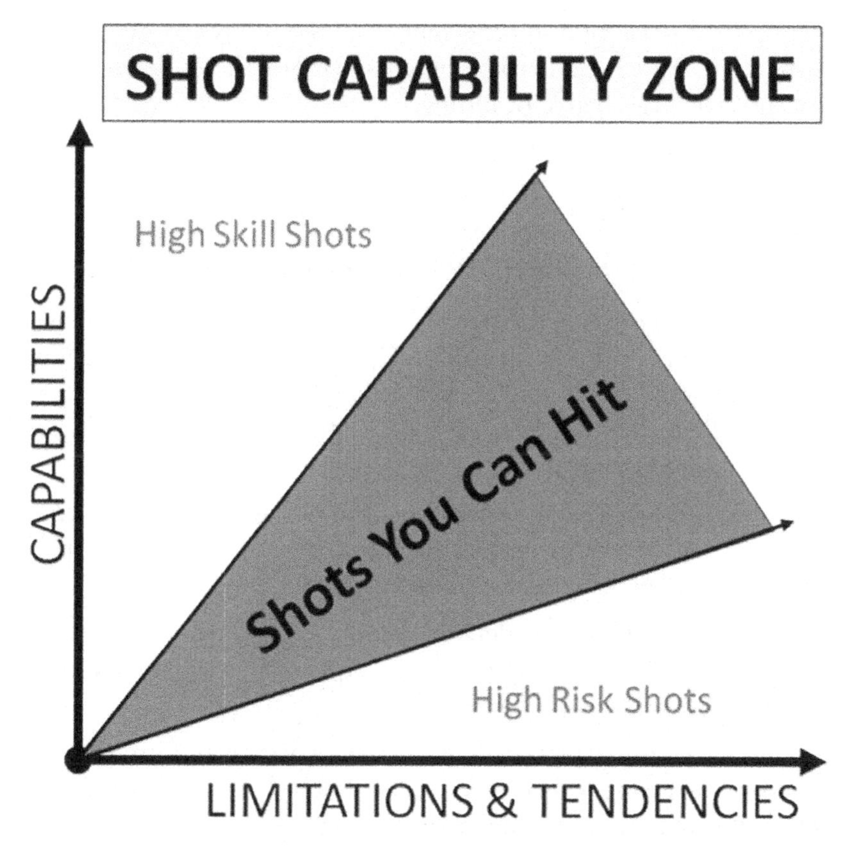

For example, nearly all golfers can hit the fairway with their driver. It's a green zone capability shot. Usually.

But if you're facing a narrow fairway and the reality is that you only hit the fairway 30% of the time, choosing driver may actually be at the edge of the high risk zone. If hazards line both sides of the fairway, the risk of adding two strokes to your score may push the shot well into the high risk category. The smarter strategy would be to choose a club that moves you solidly back within your comfortable capability zone: a fairway metal, hybrid, or even an iron.

Recognizing all you have to do is stay within your capabilities is vital to normalizing the situation. It's already a tough situation. The more routine you can make the shot, the better your odds of success. Confidence will come from the way you prepare and train. When you've done it in practice, you'll know you can execute under stress.

You don't have to hit a miracle shot. You don't have to pull a rabbit out of a hat. To be the hero in clutch situations all you have to do is hit a shot you are capable of hitting.

You just have to do it under pressure.

Obviously it is not easy.

Insight 3: Follow a Process/Routine

Athletes who consistently perform well under pressure follow a consistent *process*. Whether it is a ritual, a series of steps, or a defined pre-shot routine, clutch players consistently use a specific process to get themselves into the best position – physically, emotionally, and mentally – to be successful.

Purposefully built pre-shot routines bring together all the clutch skills, and help you perform at the peak of your abilities. It is the routine that enables focus, commitment, rhythm and automaticity.

Tour players spend a considerable amount of time on their routines. Far more than most amateurs. They purposely design their routines to produce the results they want.

They also regularly practice their routine. They train with deliberate intention, repeating every step in the same order with the same tempo and rhythm, until it becomes second nature.

Then they stress-test their routine by simulating on-course play and pressure situations. They repeat their routine with every shot on the range and on the course. They consciously pay attention to what works best.

Your task is to design a routine with the skills that works best. Then practice that routine until it becomes a well-learned behavior you can execute automatically.

The Clutch Golfer Formula was developed specifically to help you do exactly that: create a repeatable routine that will automatically get you in the best position to perform, regardless of the situation.

Take advantage of your natural ability to automate repetitive actions by making your routine consistent. Learn what you are capable of doing under normal circumstances, and then learn to do it under pressure. Practice your routine on the range until it is automatic when you play. A consistently executed routine will put you in the best position to consistently hit your best shot in key situations.

Insight 4: Deliberately Develop Clutch Skills

Being clutch is about becoming more skilled. We all have natural abilities. Skills, on the other hand, are learned behaviors that stem from your abilities. Skill levels determine how well you perform to the limits of your abilities. Skill levels change, abilities don't.

Clutch players train to improve their skill levels in order to take maximum advantage of their abilities. They pay particular attention to the performance skills that help them perform best in pressure situations. They improve their skills through deliberate practice, performance training, and transfer training.

Being clutch requires more than developing better swing technique. Clutch players cultivate performance skills such as focus, trust, resiliency, confidence, awareness, automaticity, self-coaching, and emotional management. They deliberately work on the performance skills that help them think clearly, focus better, and execute under any circumstances.

Technique is certainly important. But coming through in a clutch situation isn't about suddenly having better technique. As Kirk Triplett said in his clutch interview:

> *"Clutch is not all of a sudden I can hit a 3-iron 15 yards farther and 10% higher and carry a hazard and stop it next to a back pin."*

That just doesn't happen.

That's why it's so important to deliberately practice performance skills that facilitate execution. Putting pressure on your shots in practice by imagining real-life scenarios allows you to continuously stretch your execution skills. Variable shot-making under pressure should be a regular staple of your practice sessions. Practicing one shot at a time, under pressure, will make you familiar with the way you respond best, so that you can then execute under pressure on the course.

Practice your playing skills. Do what you are capable of doing. Deliberately cultivate your performance skills. Follow a consistent routine. Practice under pressure. There is virtually no limit to your ability to master your performance in pressure situations.

The Difference between Practice, Training, and Execution

As McCarron's story points out, the *way* you spend your range time is more important than the amount of time. Not all practice activities are created equal. Different activities produce different results, and have different impacts on your game. Breaking your range session time into activity types will super-charge your practices. The simplest way to delineate the difference between practice, training and execution is by the outcome:

- ***Practice*** to change (technique, add skills)
- ***Train*** for performance (consistency, repetition)
- ***Execute*** for score (transfer training, simulated play)

PRACTICE	PERFORMANCE TRAINING	EXECUTION
Fundamentals, Technique Change, Add New Skills, Impact, Center Contact, Path, Face, Speed, Posture, Aim, Tempo, Rhythm	Metrics, Fairways Hit, Putts Made, Scrambling %, Approach Proximity, Lateral Accuracy, Distance Control, Trajectory, Consistency	Simulated Play, Full Routine, Variable Shots, Constraint-Based, Target Focus, Under Pressure, Competition, Mental Performance Skills

PRACTICE: The goal of practice is to discover a change for the better. Any time you try to improve your technique, change your swing, learn something new, improve specific skills, experiment, test alternatives, or fix a problem, you are in practice mode.

When you are trying to make a swing change, you are practicing. Practice is about altering, modifying, adjusting, correcting, tweaking, fixing, designing, creating, developing and building. The objective of practice is change. Not consistency, and not scoring.

Practice activities have their place. There's always something in your technique that can be improved. Unfortunately, though, practice tends to be the far too dominant activity on the range. As a rule, no more than 50% of your range time should be allocated to practice activities. The closer you are to a competition, the less time spent on practice and the more time on training and execution. Your range time will be far more beneficial to your game by balancing your practice between activities.

TRAINING: Unlike practicing, training isn't about change. Training puts the emphasis on results by counting or measuring. Consistency improves when the performance measurements improve. Whenever you are measuring results, you are in performance training mode.

Metrics are the key to performance training. Examples include counting the number of putts you can make from six feet in 10 attempts, or the number of drives you can hit into a 25-yard wide fairway, or the percentage of times you can get up and down from 5 yards off the green. The initial measurement establishes a baseline for a predetermined number of attempts (often a set of 10 tries). In subsequent 10-ball sets, the goal is to establish new performance milestones.

Establish a baseline performance level, then work on leveling up. Improve your metrics, and you'll play more consistently at a higher level. If your baseline score is five putts made from six feet, and through training you improve that to making seven, you've improved your consistency. The results will show up in more putts made on the course.

Metrics used in training can be either objective measures (like the six-foot putt example), or internal measures (subjective scales). How well would you grade your target retention on a shot, on a scale of 1 to 10? Was your focus a level 8 or higher on every shot of a three-hole, simulated play drill? Any performance skill can be graded on a subjective scale, and then trained to a higher level.

Students find performance training to be more fun and rewarding than endless tinkering with technique. Measuring improvement over time makes the effort rewarding because improvement can be tracked.

There are times, though, when the only way to reach the next higher performance level will be to make a swing change. When that happens, drop out of training mode and switch to practice mode. Make the corrections, then shift back into training mode and immediately measure how well the fix helped.

EXECUTION: Execution practice is about transferring playing skills from the range to the course. The focus is on improving your ability to score. Golf is the only sport where you don't practice in the same place you play. Simulating on-course play on the range, creating realistic scenarios, and hitting shots you are likely to see when you play, improves your readiness to succeed on the course.

For that reason, execution training is usually performed one shot at a time. Full routine, full focus. Different clubs, different targets, different shapes. As Dr. Albaugh explains in *Winning the Battle Within*, activities such as 1-ball practice, variable shot practice, playing imaginary holes, 9-ball challenge, full-routine target practice, and most forms of competition improve your ability to execute on the course.

Transfer training is about mastering the *process* of executing. It includes training your performance skills: focus, intention and trust, until they are automatic. Deliberately practicing performance skills on the range transfers to an ability to execute in competition. Add simulated pressure to make it clutch training.

In our observation, amateur golfers spend far too much time on the range in practice mode. In other words, tinkering with their technique. When there is too much emphasis on changing and fixing, without a balance of training and execution practice, the result will be inconsistent play. Quality practice balances time, emphasis, and activities, blending practice, training, and execution.

Coach's Advice

1. Do what you can do. Select shots that are within your capabilities, and be confident you'll perform to your statistical average.
2. Prepare to face challenging situations you'll see on the course, like McCarron does, by practicing playing skills, adaptability, and shot-making skills under pressure.
3. Deliberately improve your proficiency levels at the performance skills that help you most.
4. Don't think, just do. Develop a routine, practice it until you can execute automatically, then follow it consistently.
5. Divide your time judiciously between practicing, training and executing, and resist the temptation to rely solely on better technique to improve your game.

SECTION 2
HOW CLUTCH ARE YOU?

Chapter 4: The Four Pillars of Clutch

The abilities and skills used to thrive in pressure situations are common across all sports. The ever-fiercer competition at the highest professional levels has forced coaches and organizations to develop systems to deliberately and methodically refine their athletes' performance skills, just to keep pace. Seattle Seahawks coach Pete Carroll, a former student of Dr. Albaugh's, identified key building blocks of high performance and organized them into a series of steps. The steps follow a process that is at the heart of the Seahawks culture: the path to excellence.

Pete Carroll's Seahawks Win Super Bowl XLVIII

The 48th Super Bowl pitted the Seattle Seahawks against the Denver Broncos. It was a matchup of the league's leading defense vs. the league's leading offense. The Seahawks got off to the fastest start in Super Bowl history, pinning a safety on the Broncos when Peyton Manning mishandled the snap on the first play from scrimmage.

Within 12 seconds of the opening kickoff the Seahawks led 2–0, and they never looked back.

The Seahawks defense dominated the game. They caused four fumbles and recovered two. They intercepted Manning twice, returning both for touchdowns. They held the Broncos running game to just 27 yards. The final score was 43–8, one of the largest winning margins in history.

Getting a safety on the first play of the game turned out to be a clutch play. It created momentum for Seattle, and set the tone that determined the outcome of the game.

Clutch plays can come at any moment. Just getting your first drive of the day into the fairway can be a clutch shot that sets the momentum for your round. Be ready when a clutch situation arises. Coach Carroll's teams are ready for any situation because of the way they prepare. The mindset of striving for excellence – getting better every day – was established the moment Coach Carroll took over the team and is still at the core of the Seahawks culture.

Pete Carroll's Path to Excellence

We interviewed Coach Carroll for the **Clutch Interviews** to get his perspective on performance. Carroll spoke eloquently about their quest for excellence, and what it takes to perform at the highest levels over a sustained period. He outlined a very clear path to excellence and a higher level of play.

Carroll's central key to execution is focus. But focus comes from trust, and trust stems from confidence, which in turn is developed through preparation. It's a process. The steps making up the process represent the Seahawks path to excellence:

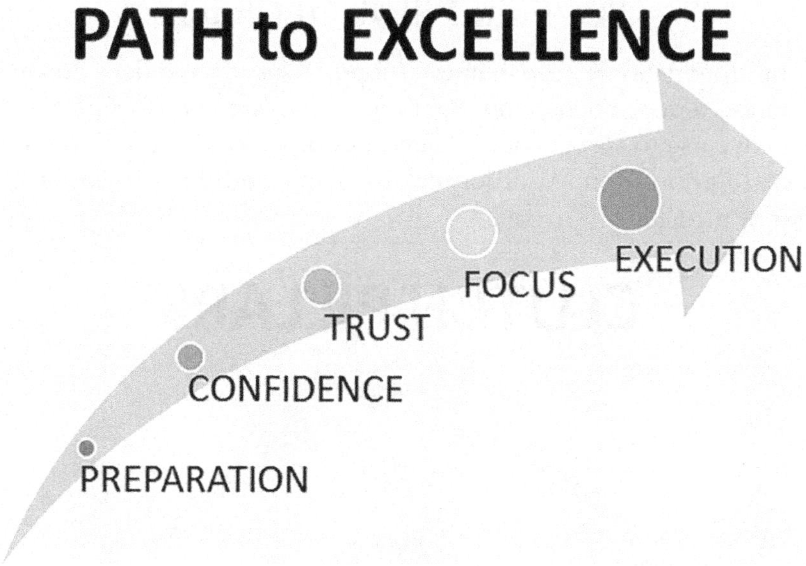

PATH to EXCELLENCE

PREPARATION

CONFIDENCE

TRUST

FOCUS

EXECUTION

> *"Really good preparation leads to confidence in your own ability. When you are confident then you can have trust, and it is trust that opens up doorways so that you can supremely focus. That's so crucial because when you have trust you can avoid discursive thoughts and concerns and you can stay focused through the challenge of the moment. That's when you have a chance to perform like you're capable, and that's all we ever shoot for."*

Coach Carroll and the Seahawks have a simple mantra for long-term success – Strive for Excellence:

> *"We strive for excellence in every moment: excellence in our thinking; excellence in our preparation; excellence in our decision-making," said Carroll. "That is what leads to excellence in execution, because all the little moments eventually add up to the big moments down the line."*

The path to clutch, like the path to excellence, features four key building blocks. The foundation of clutch play is *deliberate practice.* Deliberate practice builds confidence, which leads to *trust.* With trust comes the ability to *focus.* To supremely focus in clutch situation, we add the element of *intention.*

The Four Pillars Of Clutch

Four foundational capabilities support success under pressure: Practice, Trust, Focus, and Intention. They are the operative skills that give rise to sustained, high-level performances. They are the four skills to prioritize on your journey to clutch, and they are an integral part of the Clutch Formula.

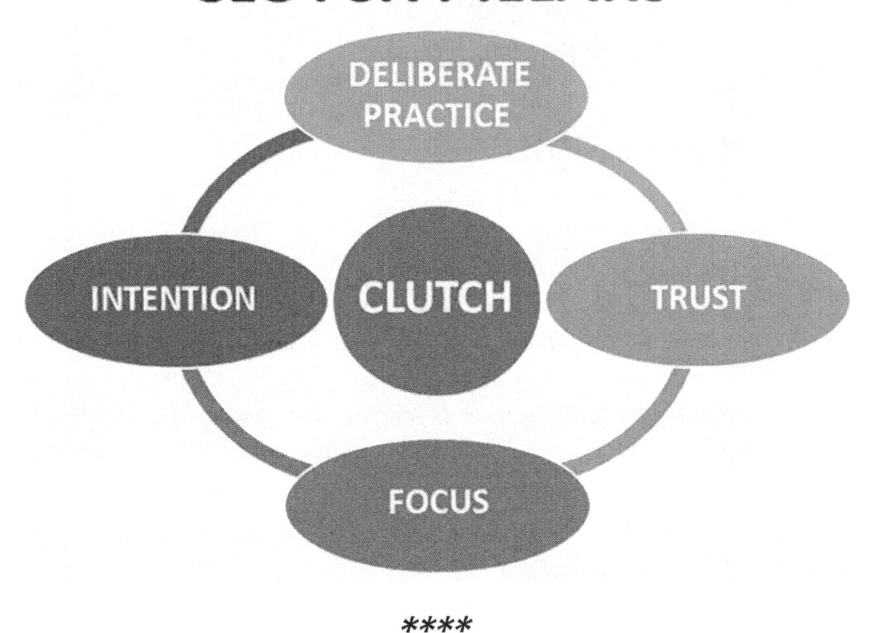

****

Clutch Pillar 1: Deliberate Practice

Anders Ericsson coined the phrase *deliberate practice* while studying elite performers and the methods they used to reach expert level performance. He found that the *way* you practice is far more important than the amount of *time* you practice.

The pop culture idea of 10,000 hours to expert status isn't quite accurate. It is more appropriately stated as ten thousand hours of highly structured practice, with intense concentration focused on deliberately using feedback to purposefully improve performance.

DELIBERATE PRACTICE

"Structured practice with intense concentration focused on deliberately using feedback to purposefully improve performance."

In his study, Ericsson observed expert musicians practicing difficult musical phrases. They slowly and methodically repeated the movements until they could place each finger exactly where it needed to be, at precisely the right moment in the sequence. Each movement was scrutinized and meticulously rehearsed until it could be accomplished with precision. Only after the movement was mastered did the musicians add speed.

Clutch players deliberately focus on practicing to improve the precision of their execution. Then they train to execute under game-time conditions. Expert performers are masters of self-coaching, developing self-awareness through self-discovery, using feedback to deliberately and purposely improve.

When it comes to developing trust, the one key activity consistently mentioned by every player, coach, and guru we interviewed is *preparation.* The common thread to developing the ability to execute under pressure is simulating the situations and shots they will face in competition, then practicing with intention. Pete Carroll said:

> *"It's the preparation – well before you ever get to the decision – that's most important. Preparation allows you to click into clear mode, let the distractions slip away, make a decision, and go for it. And once you go, you go."*

The more consistently you practice variable shots on the range, the more reliably you'll make good shots in pivotal moments on the course. Practicing the shots you expect to see on the course, and learning to execute them reliably under pressure on the range, will prepare you to perform under pressure when you play. The four pillars of clutch golf provide a framework to identify the skills you need.

The most effective way to develop those skills is through deliberate practice. Practice one skill at a time, paying meticulous attention to feedback the way Ericsson's musicians did. Practice at a speed that allows you to refine your execution with precision. Add speed as the skill is mastered and integrate it into the shot sequence until it can be executed automatically.

****

Clutch Pillar 2: Trust

Webster's Dictionary says that trust is "*An assured reliance on ability … a behavior in which confidence is placed … to do something without fear or misgivings … a deep belief in one's ability.*"

Clutch players trust their swing. Trust is built through consistent repetition of quality contingency practice and inner-game drills, as Dr. Albaugh points out in his book *Winning The Battle Within.* It is reinforced through conscious execution on the golf course.

Trust is at the peak of the athletic performance pyramid. Planning ensures you are working on the right things. Practicing the right way builds belief. Preparation equips you to perform, and peak performances are built on trust, allowing you to make your most athletic swing with freedom.

Trust is also the foundation of automaticity. When you trust your swing and your capabilities, you can let your swing go without conscious thought or emotional interference. Performing without interference allows you to play at your best.

It doesn't need to be perfect. There are as many "perfect swings" as there are golfers. As Dr. Albaugh states in *Winning the Battle Within*: "The perfect swing is the one you trust. You will be surprised at how effective your swing will become, no matter how unorthodox, once you decide to trust it. There is virtually no limit to your improvement as a golfer when learning to trust your swing becomes a priority."

Trust, though, can be elusive. Many golfers, particularly those who seek improvement through the latest swing fixes and equipment offerings, fail to find it. Lasting trust is not something you find or buy: it is something you develop within yourself.

As Coach Carroll said, if you have trust you can focus, and when you can focus you can execute to the height of your abilities.

Trust is built through preparation. It is tempered in the fires of competition. It is honed to a fine edge through the crucible of clutch performances.

Clutch Pillar 3: Focus

Focus is one of the most important skills for success in any endeavor. The ability to concentrate by paying selective attention, or by directing attention to a specific objective, keeps athletes centered in the moment and capable of playing to their ability. Maintaining focus is a critical element of peak performance.

Like looking through a camera lens, focusing brings the target into crystal clarity, along with the shot that will get your ball there. Everything else becomes a blur.

Focus, however, is not an all-or-nothing, on/off switch. There are various degrees. On stock shots under normal conditions you may get away with being less than 100% focused. Difficult shots require more concerted focus. When it comes to pressure situations, simply reaching a high level of focus can be exceedingly difficult, and sustaining it even more so.

A natural reaction to stress is to become hyper-aware. Our instinctive fight/flight reflex compels us to take in as much information as possible to evaluate all potential threats, whether real or imaginary. The tendency under stress is to become *too* aware of outside influences, thoughts, and emotions. It's too much information for our limited short-term memory to process effectively.

The skill of managing focus lies in reversing the natural reaction to pressure. Instead of a broad focus, zero in with narrow, laser-sharp clarity. Under pressure, it's like going from a wide-angle lens to telescopic zoom.

It takes appreciable energy to maintain a high level of focus. Higher states of focus, though, are associated with higher levels of play:

- Optimal focus means paying selective attention only to the appropriate environmental cues, and generally results in a higher level of execution. The challenge is to determine which specific cues are relevant to performance, and then to disregard everything else.
- Total focus is an even higher state, where the athlete is completely absorbed in the task at hand, present-centered in the moment, and in tune with their actions. Athletes execute at their highest levels when they have total focus, and often experience Zone or flow-like performances.

The words that describe focus are also the skills used to control it: paying attention, concentrating, clarity, exerting effort, directing energy to a goal, zeroing in, and narrowing vision. Improving execution of these focusing skills takes conscious effort, self-awareness and mindfulness. When it's your turn to hit, use these skills to narrow your focus and become:

- Task specific
- Centered in the present time
- Concentrated on the task at hand
- Fully engaged in the moment

Narrowing your focus to a specific task and target gives you the ability to manage over-thinking, eliminate conscious control, and reduce emotional interference. High level focus will help to:

1. Cement the target in your mind's eye so that you retain target awareness all the way through impact
2. Diffuse unnecessary thoughts, emotions, and distractions

Your focus will go up and down throughout the round. You don't need to be as focused in between shots as you do over the ball. Thus the ability to regulate focus will play a critical role in your performance.

Many performance-specific techniques can be used to assist with focus. Three of the most common techniques are Relaxation Breathing, Visualization, and Positive Self-Talk. Any or all three of them can be used to control your focus. They help with concentration, attention, effort, clarity, and control.

Experiment with focusing skills as you develop your own personalized clutch golfer formula. Determine which techniques and skills best help you achieve a clutch level of total focus, and integrate them into your routine.

****

Clutch Pillar 4: Intention

Intention means clearly and specifically deciding in advance the result you want, and then deliberately and willfully setting out to accomplish it. Intention is "*an anticipated outcome that guides your planned actions*"(vocabulary.com). Make up your mind about what you intend to have happen. See the target and the shot in advance. Take deliberate aim. Execute your intention with commitment.

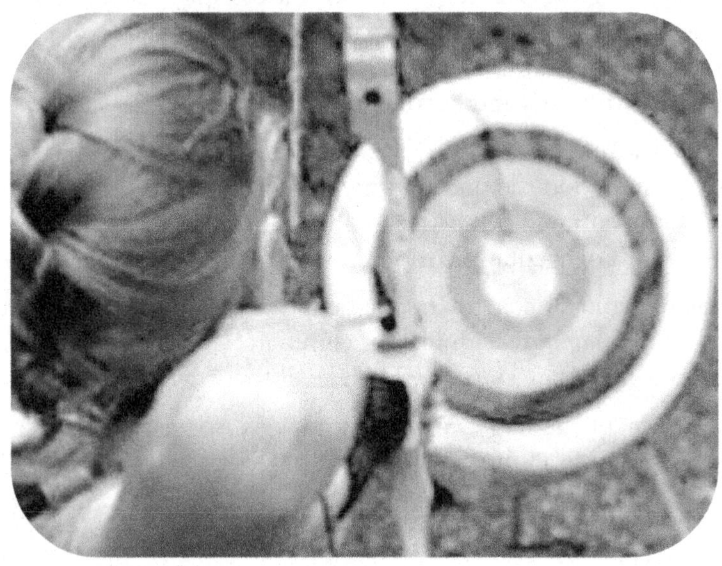

Intentional golf shots are very purposeful. In a tight situation, you don't have the luxury of waiting until you are playing well to hit a good shot. You have to make a specific shot happen – by design and on purpose – and you need it now.

Specificity of intent matters. An intent to *hit the green* is not as specific as *fading a soft 7 to a spot 15 feet below a back right pin*. The more specific the intent, the easier it will be to remain focused and committed.

Strangely enough, there are shots where your options are so limited, it can be unexpectedly easy to focus, no matter how challenging the situation. Like punching out of the rough through a narrow opening: there's only one place the ball can go. It's clear what has to happen.

When the shot can be visualized with such specificity, the singular intention frees you up to execute without reservation. It's surprising how often we pull off those shots. The caveat is that it works best for shots you have practiced and know you can hit.

These shots illustrate why clarity is so critical, and why intention is a significant component of confidence. When you can clearly imagine the shot, you have a better chance of hitting it. The more clearly you can see and feel the shot, the more confidence you'll have.

The most challenging aspect of sticking with your intention is resisting the temptation to control your swing. It is hard to let go. It's even harder on tough shots.

Crucial situations call for putting aside swing thoughts and abandoning the idea of micromanaging your swing. When it is time to execute, there is no thinking. Just doing.

It's not easy, but that's where routines help. Your routine will help you remain committed to your intention and allow you to execute on automatic, unimpeded by mental or emotional interference.

Combining intention with intense narrow focus allows you to be single-minded. Maintaining commitment keeps you fully engaged until the end of the shot, allowing you to swing with confidence and trust. When it comes time to make the pivotal shot that counts – be clear on your intention, and maintain it throughout the swing.

****

To gauge your skill level at the four clutch pillars, take the Clutch Test in the next chapter.

Coach's Advice

1. Engage in deliberate practice. The *way* you practice is far more important than the amount of *time* you practice.
2. Practice in ways that builds trust, particularly by emphasizing performance and execution training.
3. Develop the ability to regulate your focus throughout your round, and be prepared to kick it up to a high gear on pivotal shots.
4. Have a clear strategy for your shot, and be intentional about achieving it.
5. Use techniques like relaxation breathing, visualization, and positive self talk to augment pillar skills.

Chapter 5: The Clutch Test

In compiling our research on clutch, our qualitative analysis revealed a consistent set of skills described by top players. The skills generally fell into one of four categories: practice, trust, focus, and intention. Virtually all clutch shots employed some or all of these skills.

We then designed a series of questions to probe golfers' subjective assessments of their skill levels and habits in these four categories. The more these four skills are present during the shot, the greater the probability of success. That is to say, the better your practice prepares you for the shot, and the greater your ability to sustain trust, focus and intention, the more likely you are to succeed.

Bobby Clampett provided a great example in his Clutch Interview with a very detailed account of his clutch shot and the process he used. He'd practiced the shot so he trusted that he could hit it, and his visualization was so clear that he attained a very high level of focus and intention. All four skill categories were present at a high level.

Bobby Clampett: A State of Hyper-Focus

Bobby Clampett dominated the amateur golf scene from 1978 to 1980. He was a three-time All-American at Brigham Young University and twice won the Fred Haskins Award winner for College Player of the Year. He was the low amateur at the 1978 U.S. Open as well as the 1979 Masters, and was the Amateur Golfer of the Year in 1978, winning the World Amateur Medal. He won a record 12 college tournaments and was inducted into the BYU Hall of Fame.

Clampett faced many pivotal moments in compiling his stellar amateur record. In his clutch interview, Clampett described one shot in particular that marked a turning point and ultimately led to a long career on the PGA and Champions Tours. It's the shot where he realized, as he put it,

> *"If my focus and concentration is keen enough I can do just about anything."*

That moment – which he still recalls vividly – was his third shot on the 18th hole in the semifinals at the 1979 U.S. Amateur.

Clampett came in on a hot streak, with wins at the Western Amateur, Porter Cup, Western Junior, and California State Championship. His hot play continued in qualifying, where he posted a 66 in the first round and set a new course record at Canterbury Golf Club that still stands to this day. He followed that with a 68 at Shaker Heights to win U.S. Amateur Medalist honors by four shots.

In the semi-finals, Clampett faced longtime friend and college rival (and future PGA Tour player) Gary Hallberg. In a grueling match, Clampett was one-down coming into the final hole. He had to win the 18th just to extend the match.

Hallberg's drive found the middle of the fairway. Clampett, on the other hand, got off to an inauspicious start when his drive kicked into the heavy rough. Hallberg's second shot was a beautiful 4-iron that landed on the green 15 feet from the hole. The best Clampett could do on his second was hack a 5-wood out of the rough, knocking it into the rough short of the green.

With Hallberg on in two and Clampett still 40 yards away, it looked like the match was over. Either Clampett holed out, or the match was over. But Clampett was determined. He recalls getting into a zone he called:

> *"a state of hyper-focus and tunnel vision. I saw the ball going into the hole from 40-50 yards out of the rough."*

It was a tough shot that required seeing much more than just the ball going in the hole. Clampett used his considerable imagination skills to evaluate a myriad of variables beforehand:

> *"The ball was in the deep rough. I had to visually figure out how the club was going to come through the grass, how much interference the grass was going to create with the ball, and how the grass would affect the shot, so how much harder than normal I'd have to hit that shot."*

Hyper-focus allowed Clampett to construct such a meticulously detailed mental image of the shot that he could literally feel every aspect of the swing aim and impact before it happened.

> *"I've always said that the three most important things on a golf shot are to execute, execute, and execute. Execution starts with all the left brain stuff beforehand. The evaluation of the lie with the club selection. The hole position. The strategy. Then it shifts into the right brain stuff and the shot: visualizing the curvature of the ball and its trajectory, and also what that perfect strike at impact feels like."*

Trust emerges when the mind and body are in such perfect sync that execution happens automatically.

> *"Then executing is trusting your swing and your mechanics: letting your brain go there, and using all your senses in a positive way to experience it. That to me is what the game is all about."*

Bobby hit the shot he so vividly imagined. His club sliced through the grass exactly as he calculated. The ball came out, landed on the green, and rolled right across into the hole. The match was extended.

Take the Clutch Test

Although every situation is different, four fundamental skills – ***focus, intention, trust, and practice*** – are the foundational pillars of sustained clutch performance. The Clutch Test measures skill levels within each of the pillars. By answering a series of 20 questions, you'll gain insights into your strengths and weaknesses, as well as a rating of your overall likelihood of success in clutch situations.

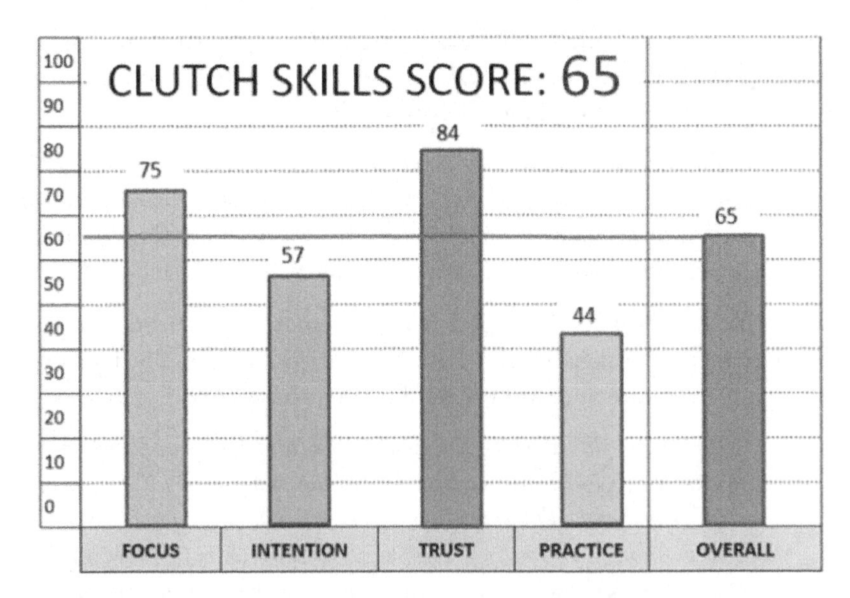

We invite you to take the Clutch Test online. It's free, it's fun, and it's insightful. To find your own level of clutchness visit iGolfU.com/ClutchTest, create a Student Account at iGolfU, and enroll in the Clutch Test.

Your results will be emailed to you once you submit the 20-question survey. The graphical format provides an instant snapshot of areas of strength as well as areas that would benefit from attention.

Interpreting Your Clutch Test Results

The Clutch Test provides a baseline assessment of performance skills. Your overall results will give you an indication of how often you could expect to succeed in clutch situations. If you want to succeed more often, improve your clutch skill levels.

Use the test results to set goals for your game. The overall test results make it intuitive to identify the broader skills to address. Then look within each pillar to examine scores on specific questions regarding skills, habits and practices. Your individual question score will help you prioritize practice activities as well as allocate enough time to each of them.

Whenever possible, make notes in a journal when you practice and play. We encourage you to take the test again after some period of time, once you have practiced and implemented changes, to measure progress and readjust your goals.

Focus Skills Analysis

Accomplishing your objective under pressure requires the ability to maintain a narrow, specific and unwavering focus throughout the shot. That's clutch focus. It is present-centered, in the moment, and exclusively on the task at hand.

When you have clutch focus, the target, shot and feel of the swing are crystal clear. Everything else fades into the background. Building a step in your routine to narrow your focus to a specific task and target will help you manage interference from conscious control and emotional overload.

Golfers who score higher in Focus:

- Narrow their focus to only what matters
- Have a clear and specific target on every shot
- Maintain target focus throughout their routine and through impact
- Are aware of the situation and circumstances surrounding their shot
- Are aware of their capabilities and limitations (self-awareness)
- Are present-centered and focused solely on the task at hand
- Use their pre-shot routine to both sharpen focus and minimize distractions
- Keep the present shot at the forefront of their minds
- Have techniques to deal with distractions and interference

Golfers who score lower in Focus:

- Have difficulty freeing themselves from swing thoughts
- Allow emotions to affect their swing
- Do not always have a clear, well thought-out shot strategy
- Are negatively affected by outside distractions
- Do not consistently use a pre-shot routine
- Focus on the outcome and score, rather than execution
- Are not present-centered in the moment and on the task at hand

- Have minimal awareness of the situation and circumstances surrounding their shot
- Cannot let go of past shots or are anxious about future outcomes
- Split their focus in multiple directions instead of on the task at hand
- Allow pressure to affect their decision-making process and/or swing
- Lose their target awareness somewhere during their swing

There are five questions that address specific focus-related skills. Investigate your answers to individual questions to identify specific skills that will help you achieve a higher level of focus, then practice them:

1. Clarity
2. Present-centered
3. Process
4. Task focus
5. Awareness

The techniques and steps used to improve skill levels will differ for every player. A high score in focus is an area of strength. It is always advantageous to play from your areas of strength. Continue to reinforce your focusing strengths through performance training and execution drills. On the course, try to put yourself in situations where you can use your strength of getting focused.

If you scored low in focus, consider it an opportunity for rapid improvement. The skills that facilitate focus are all within your control. You can develop awareness around them, and employ numerous tools and techniques to improve them. It takes time. But it's far faster than trying to make incremental swing changes. Plus, we've observed that when golfers have a specific learning objective, they have a more enjoyable and productive experience working to achieve it.

Intention Skills Analysis

Intention combines clarity of purpose with deliberate action. To be intentional, clearly determine your target, shot and club, commit to your strategy, and then deliberately, purposefully, and willfully execute. Intention generates the confidence that allows your swing to go freely and automatically, unimpeded by conscious control.

Being intentional in clutch requires putting aside swing thoughts and the notion of controlling your swing. Intention also helps channel emotions. Although emotions can't be eliminated, having a firm intention enables you to manage emotional distractions in such a way that they do not interfere with your execution. As Michael Murphy wrote in *Golf in the Kingdom*, "*Get to know the invader. It'll help your game.*"

With clear intention it is even possible to turn strong emotions into productive energy, helping you remain focused and committed throughout the swing.

Golfers who score higher in Intention:

- Have clarity before they execute
- Purposefully set out to accomplish their objective
- Are confident they will get results
- Commit 100% to their decisions
- Can imagine and feel the shot before hitting
- Have a well defined pre-shot routine with the same steps and the same order
- Consistently use their pre-shot routine before each shot

- Synchronize what they see/imagine with the feel of the swing
- Let their swings go on automatic

Golfers who score lower in Intention:

- Are not clear on exactly what they want to accomplish
- Have an inconsistent pre-shot routine
- Do not use a pre-shot routine on every shot
- Have difficulty swinging with a consistent rhythm and tempo
- Don't stay fully committed to their strategy
- Hope the shot will happen vs. purposefully making the shot happen
- Second-guess their decisions

The test questions that measure intention are centered on five skills:

1. Routines
2. Purpose
3. Synchronizing
4. Will
5. Commitment

Like focusing skills, intention skills can be learned and improved. And just as with focusing skills, there are a variety of tools and techniques that can be used to facilitate the skills that contribute to intention. When it's your turn – be intentional.

Trust Skills Analysis

Trust comes from knowing what you are capable of doing, knowing what you are not capable of doing, and then selecting a strategy that fits both your game and the situation. Knowing what works best for you will keep you true to your way of playing. Trust carries a rhythm and tempo that allows you to be in tune with yourself and the moment. Belief flows from your preparation. When you have trust, you can let go.

Trusting your swing and your capabilities allows you to swing without tension. There is no need for conscious thought or emotional interference. You believe in what you can do and you make it happen. With trust you release the club with freedom and confidence, and that is when you will be the most accurate and consistent.

Golfers who score high in Trust:

- Know what they are capable of doing and not doing
- Have a firm belief in their capabilities and decisions
- Are confident in the outcome of each shot
- Let their swings release without conscious thoughts or interference
- Don't allow negative emotions to interfere with their swing
- Allow the shot to be executed automatically

- See setbacks as opportunities for growth
- Practice to deliberately develop confidence and trust
- Feel prepared for any situation
- Know how they respond mentally and physically to pressure
- Are resilient and can bounce back from setbacks

Golfers who score lower in Trust:

- Are not 100% sure of their capabilities
- Allow emotions to interfere with their swings
- Allow swing thoughts to interfere with their swings
- Second-guess their strategy or club selection
- Try to do something different in response to pressure
- Do not fully commit to their strategy
- Have difficulty swinging with confidence
- Attempt to control or micro-manage their swings
- Do not practice under simulated pressure conditions
- Don't prepare or don't feel prepared
- Are not fully aware of how their responses to pressure
- Are not resilient and cannot recover from adversity

There are five test questions that address aspects of trust:

1. Belief
2. Automaticity
3. Attitude
4. Preparation
5. Confidence

When you commit to the process of mastering clutch skills, you will develop the confidence that leads to trust. Trust is the launch pad for executing with total focus and intention.

Trust takes time, preparation, and hands-on experience to develop. When you first begin playing at a higher level, it may be easy for trust to waiver. The first time you are about to post a new career low score, it can be uncomfortable. You may not feel deserving.

Trust gives you permission to succeed and to shoot lower scores. It is earned by purposefully developing your performance skills, and by building confidence through your preparation. The higher you advance up the playing skills ladder, the more trust you acquire and demonstrate when you play. Trust is the heart and soul of clutch players.

Practice Skills Analysis

Clutch Players deliberately and intentionally merge their technique practice with performance training and with pressurized execution drills. They practice like they play, so they can play automatically on the course with focus, intention, and trust.

Learning to practice, train and execute properly is an investment you make in yourself. There are no shortcuts. Quality practice is the most efficient way to maximize your skill levels.

Golfers who score high in Practice:

- Have a clear vision of what they want to improve
- Practice with high intensity
- Practice pressure situations
- Practice to simulate on-course play
- Intentionally practice to improve skills
- Intentionally train to improve performance
- Measure the results of their practice sessions
- Practice shot-making by constantly varying targets and clubs
- Practice the process of executing
- Use a pre-shot routine on every shot – even in practice
- Use the same routine on the course that they practice on the range
- Limit the amount of time spent fixing swing technique
- Have a mastery mindset

- Practice to develop self-awareness

Golfers who score lower in Practice:

- Practice hitting the same shot over and over again
- Seldom practice under pressure
- Hit shots where there are no consequences
- Have no pre-set plan or structure for practice
- Don't connect their range session to on-course play
- Rarely practice with intensity
- Do not practice to deliberately enhance their confidence
- Constantly tinker with fixing their swing mechanics
- Do not use a routine when hitting practice shots
- Judge practice shot results as good or bad

There are five test questions that address the quality and efficiency of your practice sessions:

1. Goals
2. Measurement
3. Intensity
4. Shot-making
5. Transfer skills

The *way* you practice is more important than the amount of *time* you spend. Choose quality over quantity. Work as hard on your execution skills as you do on your technique to develop playing skills and the ability to execute under a variety of conditions.

Using the Clutch Test

The Clutch Test results will help you manage your game when you play. They also help you learn faster when you practice.

First, highlight one of the clutch pillars to address. Then explore individual test questions to identify specific skills and behaviors to assess and prioritize during practice.

If your practice sessions are not as productive as you'd like them to be – and most golfers fall woefully short in this area – your Clutch Test scores can help you determine what you should work on, and how you should work on it. Having a specific purpose for your practice sessions will make your range time not only more productive, but more fun too.

Free templates and worksheets are included in the Resources section at the end of the book. They'll help you plan and organize your practice time. Be sure to download and save the templates for your own use.

Coach's Advice

1. Take the Clutch Test to inventory your performance skills and practice habits.
2. Use the Test results to create a long-term improvement plan for your game. For short term priorities, highlight one clutch pillar, then explore individual test questions to further refine the specific skills to emphasize during practice.
3. When you are on the course, put yourself in positions where you can play from your strengths.
4. Use the Clutch Formula Template as a tool to review and select from all the skills and techniques that could be developed and integrated into your pre-shot routine.
5. Send your friends the link to the Clutch Test, then compare your results. It may lead to some very insightful discussions.

SECTION 3
THE CLUTCH GOLFER FORMULA

Chapter 6: The Clutch Formula

Routines are the heart and soul of consistent performance. You'll see them in nearly every sport: basketball players take a set number of dribbles before a free throw; place kickers take the exact same steps back and to the side for field goals; tennis players bounce and toss the ball the same way before serving. Any movement pattern that is repeated regularly will see an improvement in consistency through the use of routines.

Armed with the knowledge that focus, intention and trust are key components of high-level play, we've reached the heart of the book where we put these skills together into a routine. The Clutch Formula provides the framework.

Developing a failsafe pre-shot routine will be one of your most important tasks on the road to better golf. Following a routine you trust will be a critical factor in your ability to consistently pull off shots under pressure. Kevin Sutherland has used the same routine for more than three decades. He trusts his routine so implicitly that he never changes it, regardless of what is on the line.

Kevin Sutherland: The Million-Dollar Man

When Kevin Sutherland reached the 18th hole in the final round of the 2017 Schwab Cup Championship, he held a precarious one-shot lead. The 18th at Phoenix Country Club is a tricky par-5, dogleg right. A bunker on the right guards the corner for drives that don't carry far enough, and more bunkers line the left side for drives that carry too far. There are no safe places to miss the fairway.

The Schwab Cup is one of the biggest tournaments of the year on the Champions Tour, with one of the biggest payouts. Sutherland knew his tee shot would be the key. He had to hit a perfect drive to stay in position to secure a win.

What do you do when it feels like there's a million bucks riding on your shot? (That's exactly how much was on the line for Kevin).

You keep it simple.

You rely on a well-practiced routine tested under pressure and honed to perfection. You narrow your focus to what needs to be accomplished, make a clear decision, and then let your swing go on automatic.

In other words, as Kevin says, "You just do what you always do."

Standing on the 18th tee, Kevin knew exactly what he wanted to do. He narrowed his focus to a very precise target, visualized the shot clearly in his mind, and kept everything else simple.

> *"I aimed at the very left edge of the[corner]bunker. In my mind's eye I could see the target, and my only thought was to take this ball and put it 'there.' I didn't really think about the swing. I let my ability put the ball there with no conscious swing thought at all. It was almost like a driving range swing."*

But Kevin didn't pull off that drive by accident. He is a master at reducing the size of the moment to a manageable level. His drive split the middle of the fairway because he'd spent years training on the range, hitting shots under simulated pressure situations.

It's a key insight from Kevin: practice hitting shots under pressure on the range first, so that you'll know how to hit shots under pressure on the course.

Kevin practices one shot at a time, using his full routine, as if he were in a real competition. It's what he refers to as quality practice. He finds ways to make every shot have a consequence, so that every shot matters. Something has to be on the line.

He includes hitting different shots to different targets with different clubs. He creates different trajectories, shapes and distances. He practices different lies and conditions, including recovery shots. He practices just about every situation and shot he could imagine. He uses his full routine on every shot until it becomes as automatic as flipping a switch, regardless of the situation. Kevin's advice is simple:

> *"I always tell people 'Prepare like you play. I take what I do on the practice tee and in practice rounds, and apply that to tournament golf."*

Kevin believes that if you are not including some pressure situations in your range time, you are not going to be prepared to hit that shot in a clutch situation when it counts on the course. Pressure – even imaginary pressure on the range – makes every shot important.

Practicing under pressure, for all kinds of situations, helped Kevin develop the ability to normalize the situation. With practice, every shot can seem like just another drive, pitch, or putt. As Kevin says:

> *"I don't make that moment any different than any other moment. I just do what I always do."*

Kevin has had the same pre-shot routine for almost 35 years. He knows he can completely trust his routine under pressure.

> *"It's the same thing I did on the first hole of the first day of the first of the year. It's to the point now where it's automatic. I don't even think about it. It just happens."*

What's The One Thing Kevin Doesn't Have?

There is one thing, though, that Kevin doesn't have: mechanical or technique swing thoughts. Not when he plays, and particularly not when he is under pressure. Kevin doesn't allow swing thoughts or negative emotions to affect the way he executes. He works hard to keep it that way.

> *"I turn off my brain when I'm over the ball. I do that all the time in practice, so it just becomes a habit."*

That way he can swing "with no conscious swing thought at all – like a driving range swing."

The result?

When Kevin's moment came, he was prepared. He hit his drive down the middle of the fairway, turned the hole into a routine par, and won the Schwab Cup – plus the $1,000,000 million-dollar check.

"It was what I was expecting to happen, and that's what happened."

Wouldn't it be nice if we could all have that much confidence under pressure and just hit the shot we expected?

Sounds easy in principle. But it is very difficult to do in the heat of the moment, unless you practice clutch shots in advance and have a routine you trust.

Why Routines Are So Important

Consistent routines like Kevin's are the cornerstone of clutch performances. They evoke learned behaviors that allow your mind and body to function automatically.

Well-practiced routines inject normalcy into every situation. Familiar actions, like rituals, are a source of comfort because you know what happens next. Regardless of how the situations change, *your routine does not.* Even as the pressure mounts, you know what to expect and you already know how you'll respond. Consistent routines allow the emotional mind to disengage and thoughts to settle, while freeing the body to execute.

Pre-shot routines organize your thoughts and actions. They strengthen your connection with the shot, and then keep you focused all the way through impact. They give you clarity, which helps with intention and confidence. They ensure that your mind, body and clubface are all aimed correctly. They allow you to trust your decisions, and execute automatically.

But how do you ensure that you are bringing each aspect of focus, intention, and trust into every shot?

The simplest and easiest way to ensure you are using all the tools available to you is to develop a series of steps that deliberately call each skill and technique into play at the appropriate time. In our observation, the better the player, the more refined and purposeful the routine. High level performance requires a high level routine.

The Clutch Formula provides a detailed look at the elements that go into high-level routines, including performance enhancing skills and techniques. The best routines include a specific set-up routine that follows the same steps, in the same order, with the same tempo, and consistently take the same amount of time, every time.

Each step of your routine should be practiced until it is automatic. Consistency and automaticity are the hallmarks of well-constructed pre-shot routines, as Kevin Sutherland, Scott McCarron, Kirk Triplett and Bobby Clampett demonstrated during their clutch moments.

Action Phrases

One of the most effective ways to keep your routine consistent is to use action words and phrases.

Action words and phrases are cues used in routines to focus our attention and organize our actions. They are prompts for what we need to do, when we need to do it, and how. They are an integral part of pre-shot routines. In some cases they *are* the pre-shot routine.

Action phrases connect your athletic mind to a complete "paragraph" of movement. They can be used at any time during your routine, from behind the ball, to walking in to your set-up, to starting the swing. Action phrases typically fall into one of three different categories:

1. Instructional
2. Motivational
3. Rhythmic

Instructional action phrases tell us what to do. They are signals to begin an act or a series of familiar steps. They are also trigger words for the actions we want to take, in the order we want to take them. Examples such as *See it, feel it*, or *Ready, Aim, Fire* are instructional action phrases, telling us what to do. Each word represents multiple sub-steps, while the overall phrase keeps the process in order and in tempo.

The benefit of instructional phrases is that executing the initial cue word automatically causes the sub-steps to happen. For example, during the Lock sub-steps you'll make a conscious decision about the target, shot and strategy, see and feel the shot, get task focused, and become present-centered – all encapsulated within the mnemonic word Lock. Each of these sub-steps are themselves a process, and should be deliberately practiced until they can be executed automatically, then integrated into the overall pre-shot sequence.

Motivational action phrases spur us to a positive mindset. Phrases such as *Just Do It*, *Own it*, *You got this*, *Commit* and others reaffirm our commitment to decisions, boost confidence, and brush aside distractions, keeping the goal absolutely clear. The biggest benefits of motivational action phrases are in managing the emotional landscape, helping improve confidence, and affirming intent and commitment.

Rhythmic phrases help with tempo and feel. Scott McCarron uses *nine, nine, nine.* Sam Snead used a single word: *oily*. Another, *Low & Slow*, is both instructional and rhythmic, as is *Tee it high and let it fly.* Rhythmic phrases remind us of the flow or the feel of the swing. They synchronize what the mind sees with what the body feels. Their biggest benefit is in linking your mind with your physical senses to help with rhythm.

Action phrases help narrow focus to specific desired areas of attention. The words connect to visualization, kinesthetic awareness, body movement, swing rhythm and tempo. They affect actions, thoughts, emotions and kinesthetic feel. They are powerful contributors to automaticity.

We recommend building your initial routine around action phrases to ensure consistency and to be sure you remember all of the steps.

Jordan Spieth infamously skipped a step in his pre-shot routine and made a quadruple bogey on the 12th hole at Augusta that cost him the 2016 Masters. "*I just didn't take that extra deep breath*," he related in his post-round interview. Without it he was uncomfortable, leaving the door open for doubts to remain. He hit it into the water twice.

At Spieth's level, executing a well rehearsed pre-shot routine is just as important as executing the shot. But it is equally true for any golfer who wants to be consistent: the more reliably you execute your routine, the more consistently you'll execute the shot. Particularly under pressure.

Inside The Clutch Formula

The Clutch Formula is built around the action phrase *Lock, Load, Fire and Hold.* The phrase describes the major steps of hitting a golf shot, as well as the skills employed. The phrase helps with rhythm when repeated as a mantra: *Lock and Load, Fire and Hold.* Using the action phrase *Lock, Load, Fire, Hold* is another way to occupy your thinking and emotional minds, freeing your athletic mind to act without interference.

The Formula steps are broad enough to apply to every shot yet versatile enough for every golfer to personalize. The formula's flexibility allows it to evolve as your game evolves. The steps also provide a blueprint for identifying the skills to develop and master on the journey to clutch.

The Formula action phrase serves multiple purposes. The words are:

- Cues that engage the Thinking, Emotional and Athletic minds at the appropriate time, for the appropriate task
- Cues for the Thinking and Emotional minds to disengage

- Simple steps that are straightforward to execute. Simple is more reliable under pressure

Repeating the steps will put your swing on automatic – exactly what clutch players rely on in critical situations.

Learning to be clutch is a skill. Like any skill, it can be improved. It takes time and effort. But so does improving your swing plane or impact position.

Incorporate the four clutch pillars – deliberate practice, focus, intention and trust – into your routine. Measure the effectiveness. When you use the Formula, are you more focused? Do you maintain intention all the way through the swing? Are you swinging with trust?

There are also performance techniques, tools, and strategies – discussed below – for each step of the Formula. These performance techniques facilitate your ability to achieve focus, maintain intention, and swing with trust. If you find a technique that helps, add it to your personal clutch formula. If not, move on to a different technique.

The Clutch Golfer Formula is not about a particular style of swing or swing methodology. It is a framework for identifying, developing, and executing playing skills. You'll find that developing clutch playing skills is a faster, easier, and more enjoyable way to improve than laboring to perfect a swing motion. Playing skills are certainly more fun to teach and coach.

The Formula's four steps mirror the process golfers naturally follow to hit each shot:

1. **Lock** in to the target, the shot and the feel of the swing that matches, all in the present moment, before you step into the shot. Narrow your focus and be clear on your intention.
2. **Load** your set-up routine using the same steps, in the same order, with the same tempo and rhythm, getting centered in your most athletic ready position and aimed correctly. Slip into automatic mode.
3. **Fire** away with total commitment to your shot strategy, retaining the target and releasing without conscious or emotional interference. Maintain focus and intention, and trust your swing.
4. **Hold** your finish position to learn, reinforce, or adjust.

Below we'll examine each step in detail, explaining the goals and common techniques used.

****

Clutch Formula Step 1: Lock Your Strategy

Have a strategy.

You have to have something to lock into. Every shot begins with a strategy that fits your game and the situation. Locking in sets up all the other steps in your routine. It is difficult to load up a consistent routine and then fire away without interference if you haven't first locked in to what you intend to do and how you will do it.

Effective strategies are based on analysis, which typically starts with an evaluation of the lie, yardage, conditions and situation. Your analysis will tell you what is needed for that shot, as well as what is or isn't possible. Then you'll balance the needs of the shot against your own skills and capabilities.

For example, the shot may call for a high draw with a 7-iron to a back left pin. But if you aren't capable of hitting that shot, you may have to punch a 6-iron to the middle of the green.

Finalize your strategy by balancing what is needed against your skills and capabilities. Pick a shot you know you can hit. It is only when you are clear on a strategy that fits that you can fully lock in. Forming a strategy is also where intention begins. Focus will help you remain committed to it throughout the swing.

Sometimes, though, the situation dictates what has to happen. When the shot is do-or-die, it's pretty easy to determine the strategy. You only have one choice, so you might as well focus on it, commit to it, and let it go.

You'll see better results on *all* your shots, however, by being crystal clear on your strategy *before* you step up to the shot. That way you can focus your mind on your objective and make a decisive swing. Be intentional with your strategy.

Lock the Target and Shot

With a clear strategy you can narrow your focus until you are locked in to the shot. Create an image or feel in your mind's eye that completely describes how you will hit the ball and how it will fly to the target, including trajectory, distance, and shape. Lock into where the ball will land and how it will roll out. You are locked in when your focus narrows to nothing more than the:

- Target
- Shot
- Feel of the swing that matches what you see

Your next step is to translate the imagery in your mind into a kinesthetic sense of the shot that your body understands. That includes the choice of club, and the type of impact needed to create the shot. Rehearsal swings are the most commonly used technique. This step unites the Thinking mind with the Athletic mind so that what you see and what you feel are completely in sync.

There are many tools and techniques to help you lock in. For example:

- **Relaxation Breathing** can help you become centered in the moment on the task at hand and to move tension-free.
- **Visualization** can be used to narrow your focus by imagining the shape, trajectory and direction of the shot, letting everything fade into the background except a clear picture of the shot.
- **Positive Self Talk** that is specific to the shot and in support of a positive mindset will help with confidence, leading to trust and a focus on the successful outcome

These mental skills are just a few of the performance techniques available to help you lock in during this first step. Use your self-discovery skills to find techniques that work best for you.

The goal at the first step in the Clutch Formula is to lock in with a process that facilitates your ability to narrow your focus and become intentional – two of the clutch pillars. Locking in prepares you mentally and physically to move to the next stage where you load the swing and your set-up routine.

When you lock in, you get clear on your strategy, focused on the present shot, and in sync with the swing. That makes it easier to set up with confidence and execute automatically with trust. Lock in both mentally and physically. There is only one shot that matters: the one you are about to hit. There is only one time that matters: right now.

Consider locking in from behind the ball, where you can see both the ball and the target at the same time. From that position you can more easily picture the ball taking off and curving to the target. There you can also rehearse the swing that matches what your mind is seeing, while you are still looking at the target. It's the best position to engage all your senses while synchronizing your Thinking mind with your Athletic mind.

Start by standing behind the ball. Begin locking in by narrowing your focus until you are crystal clear on your target, shot and feel of the matching swing. Lock in to:

- A specific target at a specific location. The smaller and more detailed the target, the sharper the visual acuity
- The moment, centering your thoughts in the present, focused solely on the task at hand
- The feel of the swing and synchronize what you see with what you feel using rehearsal swings. Know exactly what you intend to do, how you intend to do it, and what it will feel like when you do it
- Your ideal emotional intensity level. Use performance management techniques to keep emotions like worry or fear from pulling your focus into the future, or emotions like frustration or anger, from diverting your focus to the past
- Your intention by reaffirming commitment to your strategy

Lock Checklist

- Analyze situation
- Pick specific target
- Imagine shot shape
- Imagine shot trajectory
- Select Strategy
- Pick club
- Narrow Focus
- Be intentional
- Commit
- Rehearse Feel
- Target Location
- Breathe
- Visualize
- Use Positive Self Talk
- Affirmations
- Centering
- Posture

****

Clutch Formula Step 2: Load

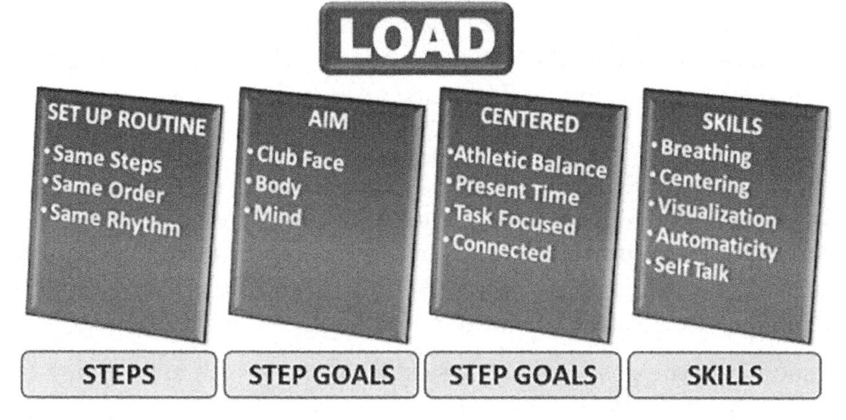

Once you are locked in, the next step in the Clutch Formula is to load your set-up routine. Your set-up routine is the process used to get in position to hit the shot. It is a subset of your overall pre-shot routine and takes place once you are clear on your strategy and have started your walk from lock to load. Move to the set-up stage only *after* you are locked in.

For many players, the set-up routine begins with the golfer standing behind the ball. It's the best position to see the target and ball at the same time. It's also the easiest position to activate your imagination and connect the ball to the target, while "seeing" what the shot will look like flying to the target.

Many players prefer to do rehearsal swings from behind the ball for this reason. Rehearsal swings synchronize what your conscious mind is imagining with what your body is sensing as it moves, while simultaneously integrating the target location. Rehearsals load the feel of the proper swing into the Athletic mind.

Coach's Note: We deliberately use the term "rehearsal" swings, not practice swings. Practice swings are what you do when you are trying to change a movement. They direct your focus inward. Rehearsal swings, on the other hand, mimic the shot you are about to hit.

Rehearsal swings usually mark the beginning of the hand-off from conscious thought to physical execution. Starting the walk to the ball completes the handoff. Approaching the ball is an action cue, a physical movement telling your conscious mind to disengage. From that point on, the routine and swing should be on automatic.

Nilsson & Marriot's ThinkBox/PlayBox idea from their book *Every Shot Must Have a Purpose* is a brilliant way to differentiate what you should be doing, where, and when. When you are behind the ball, you are in your ThinkBox. That's where you do all your thinking, strategizing, practicing, and rehearsing. But when you step into the PlayBox, all that gets left behind. Your only task in the PlayBox is to get the ball to your target.

Learning to flip the switch to disengage the conscious mind is an important part of achieving automaticity and eliminating cognitive interference during your swing. Action cues are the most common technique used to kick off the set-up routine.

Action cues are any sort of physical movement such as resetting the Velcro on your glove, tapping the ground with your club, taking a relaxation breath, hitching up your shirt sleeve, or any other kind of act. Physical action engages the Athletic mind.

As you transition from Lock to Load, follow a consistent pattern of steps, in the same order, with the same rhythm each time. Your brain recognizes familiar movement patterns and immediately reinforces the neural pathways so it can be repeated. Our bodies are hard-wired to automate repetitive processes, because it frees up the brain to focus on higher-level priorities. Automating repetitive movements is another survival trait. Not only that, once we automate a process, our hard-wired reflex is to constantly refine the process to make it as efficient, reliable, and accurate as possible.

This process is true for every repetitive movement, not just sports. The more we repeat an action, the better we get at it. With enough repetitions over time, the motions become highly consistent and accurate. As legendary sport psychologist Ken Ravizza once quipped:

> *"After all, when was the last time you missed putting a fork full of food into your mouth?"*

That's the kind of accuracy and precision we want in our golf swing.

The familiarity of well-rehearsed routines has a calming influence on emotions because the Emotional mind knows what to expect next. A familiar routine gives the Emotional mind something to anchor to and helps to minimize interference. We like familiar. We don't like change. Routines are time-tested tools for managing emotions.

Design your set-up routine to accomplish other clutch skills such as aiming correctly, being mentally present, focusing on the task at hand, and getting athletically ready to make the shot. A rhythmic walk from lock to load can even help produce a rhythmic swing.

Use positive self talk to channel your internal dialog in a helpful direction. Both supportive language and task-specific instructions help narrow and maintain focus, reinforce commitment and boost confidence.

Find your rhythm. Practice staying in rhythm. Using a waggle can help with rhythm and maintaining feel. It is an essential component of automaticity and high-level performance.

Execute your set-up process with all deliberate speed. Don't hurry, but be quick enough that the feel you developed during your rehearsal swings is still fresh as you walk up to the ball and set up. The longer you wait over the ball, the fainter your target connection becomes, and the more likely interference will creep in from conscious thoughts or emotions. Six to nine seconds, from the moment you sole your club behind the ball to the moment of impact, has been our common observation of an optimal time for the set-up process.

There's a lot to be accomplished during the set-up process. The best way to ensure every step happens is to practice your set-up routine as deliberately as you practice any other golf skills.

Practice the same steps, in the same order, at the same tempo to set up over the ball and get ready to swing. Practice it until it is automatic. Then use the same set-up routine on every shot on the golf course.

Your body's natural inclination to automate repetitive motions works in your favor, so use it to your advantage. The more you practice and repeat the same steps in the same way, the easier it will be for you to automate the load process on the course.

Load Checklist

- Action Cue (word, phrase or action): __________
- Approach the ball in rhythm
- Set Up to ball: (same steps, in order, rhythm and tempo)
- Take aim (club face, body, mind at target)
- Center mind in present
- Center body in athletic ready position
- Maintain focus
- Intention is clear
- Retain target location
- Commit
- Positive Thoughts
- Walk rhythm
- Athletic mind in sync

If your focus or intent slips or you sense interference, now is the time to address it. Step away from the ball, reacquire your target focus, reaffirm your intention, and then step back in to your set-up routine.

****

Clutch Formula Step 3: Fire

Swing!

The ultimate goal, of course, is to hit a great golf shot to your target. After locking into your target, shot, and feel and then loading your set-up process, you've completed the transfer to your Athletic mind. When in this stage there is no thinking, no worries. Your decision is made and your strategy selected. All that remains is target focus, the feel of the swing, and your intention. It's time to execute.

That's where Fire comes in.

The word "fire" evokes aggressive action. When you fire there's no going back. And when you fire with complete freedom of movement and rhythm, you wouldn't want to. You are committed. There is nothing as satisfying as letting your swing go with confidence and crushing a drive, sticking an approach shot, or holing a putt. Especially when you pull off exactly the shot you intended.

Automatic Swings

One of the key roles of the pre-shot routine is to get yourself into automatic mode. The automaticity ingrained in a well-rehearsed routine enables you to put interfering thoughts and emotions to the side. You are ready to swing when you are fully intentional, present-centered, and task focused.

It is critical to stay in that mode throughout the swing when you fire.

There is no tension in your swing when you fire on automatic. Tension occurs when there are conflicting strategy objectives. Your strategy is a single shot with a result that does not include any options. Neither should your swing.

If you are still thinking or making decisions when you are over the ball (or heaven forbid *during* your swing), then the breakdown is in your routine, not your swing. You're not as locked in, focused, and intentional as you could be.

Mechanical thoughts pull your focus away from the target and redirect it to one tiny aspect of your swing. They obscure the feel developed through rehearsal swings. They add confusion to your Athletic mind. On the one hand you've told your body to execute a complete movement with a single objective – hit the ball to the target. But when you add mechanical instructions, you suddenly give the body two objectives to accomplish, at the same time. *Hit the ball to the target, but also make sure the elbow stays down at the top.* You'll get one or the other, but seldom both.

There is no place for mechanical swing thoughts when you fire at a target. You are out there to score. On the course, results are the *only* thing that matters. The swing doesn't need to be perfect. It just has to get the job done. How your swing accomplishes the objective is irrelevant.

Firing automatically requires the conscious mind to remain disengaged throughout the entire swing. Yet the conscious mind can't do nothing. Nature abhors a vacuum. If you don't give the conscious mind a task, it will pick something to fill the void. Usually to the detriment of your shot.

Target Retention

That's where target retention and imagery come in. Rather than use internal verbal commands or mechanical instruction, allow your swing to emerge from the image and the feel.

In open-skill sports like basketball, football, baseball, soccer and tennis, athletes react to the target. Basketball players in the flow of the game don't think about their mechanics when they shoot. They focus on the rim and react, letting the body carry out the shot the way it knows best.

How many times have we seen a player fouled going up for the shot, yet still make it? They've been knocked out of position so it's not possible to execute a normal stroke. But somehow their body makes the appropriate adjustments.

The body processes millions of pieces of data per second while the conscious mind can manage one thing at a time. The body's reaction time is thousands of times faster than the conscious mind. It is simply not possible for the conscious mind to react fast enough to send new instructions to account for the shooter's suddenly altered position. Rather, it is almost as though the target reaches out to attract their focus, like a magnet. The body just responds. Retaining a target image will give your body all the information it needs. A swing that matches what you see will follow.

Intention and Trust

Maintaining intention will help you fire away with freedom. Intention is a clutch pillar. Intention facilitates commitment, confidence and control. During your strategy step, you have all the time you need to consider every possible outcome. When you fire, though, there is only one outcome. Retaining an image of the target reinforces your intention and commitment to the outcome you want.

Belief also plays a crucial role in firing automatically. Belief is at the core of trust. Trust – another pillar of clutch play – allows you to act without hesitation. The trust you build through practice, training and preparation builds your internal confidence with belief in your capabilities. Trust enables you to fire your swing with conviction.

When you are ready to fire, center yourself to start in balance, stay in balance and finish in balance. Stay mentally balanced in the present as well. Maintain target awareness. Keep your swing in sync with your pre-shot image. Trust the swing you have all the way to the end of your finish. Stay focused and intentional, no matter the circumstances.

Believe in your decisions, trust your process, and let your swing happen without interfering. Firing should happen so automatically that you have very little conscious awareness of your actions. Your focus should be so intense that all you are tuned into is the shot and how you want it to turn out. If you're properly locked in and set up, there is nothing left to do but swing freely. Adding anything else would only interfere. Let your body carry out the motions you know it can do. Fire away.

Skill Review

That said, there are a number of skills happening when you swing and several step goals to review once the swing is over.

You should transition into the Fire stage with focus, intent and confidence, already in place from your Lock and Load steps. You should exit the Fire step the same way you came in.

Focus and belief should be unwavering. When the swing is over, assess your execution on these skills and how well you were able to:

- Remain focused
- Stay committed to your intention
- Retain the target
- Swing in rhythm
- Maintain trust
- Execute without interference

Caution: Consciously evaluating your focus, intention and trust while you swing will cause interference. So will monitoring your thoughts, or your emotions, or your swing mechanics. Unless you are at the range or playing a practice round, evaluation, monitoring and instructions should not be part of your swing. Practice is the appropriate time to assess your skill levels on these critical mental processes. In competition the goal is execution without interference.

There's a lot of information available to you when you swing. It is up to you to make sure that nothing interferes when you fire. Learn it, then learn to let it go.

Fire like you mean it.

Fire Checklist

Focus and belief should be unwavering. When the swing is over, assess your execution on these skills and how well you were able to:

- Remain focused
- Stay committed to your intention
- Retain the target
- Swing in rhythm
- Maintain trust
- Execute without interference
- Finish tall

Clutch Formula Step 4: Hold

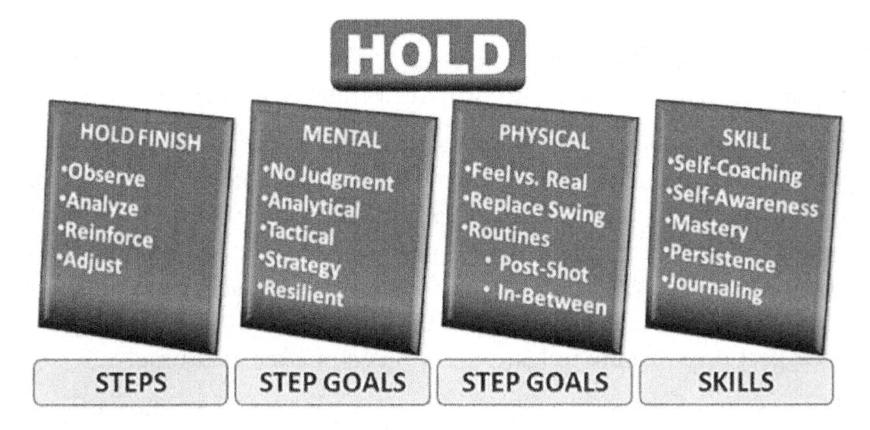

Here's a question we pose to new students: "When does learning take place: before, during, or after the shot?"

The answer: All learning takes place *after* the shot.

If you don't take a moment after the shot to process the results, you miss your best opportunity to learn from it and make adjustments.

When the shot is over, we recommend holding your finish position for a few seconds – at least long enough to process the shot while the ball is in the air and landing. You can watch the shot and receive some feedback from impact, but you only learn from it after the swing is over.

You only have a few seconds to process the physical feedback from your shot. Just as our body is hard-wired to automate repetitive motions, it is also hard-wired to forget physical input as quickly as possible. If it didn't, we would be overwhelmed with the constant barrage of data from all our senses.

A few seconds is enough time to reflect on the feel of the swing and the moment of impact. It is also time enough to evaluate your mental process and emotional state. Whether it is on the course or on the range, those few seconds after the shot will be your best opportunity to learn from what just happened. It is when your Thinking, Emotional, and Athletic minds are in harmony.

Your Post-shot Routine

Like a pre-shot routine, your post-shot routine is a series of steps executed consistently after each shot. They direct your attention to the appropriate feedback and provide a framework for analysis.

Hold also includes action steps to either reinforce the swing or make adjustments. Your best opportunity for self-coaching will come from your post-shot routine, both when you are playing on the course and practicing on the range. Holding your finish for a few seconds gives you time to analyze the shot, reflect on the impact, recapture your swing feel, and catalog your thoughts and emotions. Used wisely, it is your best opportunity to learn and do even better next time.

The results of the shot will provide data for your post-shot analysis. Impact, direction, and trajectory provide the physical feedback. Focusing attention internally will provide the feedback on mental performance. Were you totally absorbed in the moment, or was there interference? Did you lose focus, doubt your strategy, or question your abilities? Were focus and intention the same after you fired as they were before?

Use self-discovery skills to note physical and mental tendencies. Catalog trends and add them to notes in your journal. Turn your observations into stats, which you can later use to plan training sessions and measure progress.

Avoid judging shots. Judging injects emotion into the results, which interferes with learning. Suspending judgment is a learned behavior. By analyzing the results as merely data, without judging them as good or bad, you have an opportunity to improve. The better your skill at suspending judgment, the more effectively you'll manage emotions.

Evaluate your skill at remaining committed to your strategy all the way through impact, locked in to the target location, shot, and club. Then use positive self-talk to channel your internal dialog in a productive direction.

Post-Shot Routine Action Steps

Holding your finish a few seconds is also the best time to take one of the two action steps we recommend after the shot:

1. Adjust, or
2. Reinforce

Adjust: If the result of the shot was not what you intended, your post-shot routine should include a correction swing. Watch Tour players and you'll see many of them recreate their swing immediately after hitting an errant shot. They are not fixing their swing; they are fixing their execution. Did I execute the right feel? Have the right strategy? Keep the target image? Stay in rhythm? Remain committed? Release without interference?

A missed shot, if not immediately attended to, can affect the rhythm of your round. If you miss a shot, take a moment in your post-shot routine to make the proper swing you originally intended. It is a chance to overwrite the mishit with the feel of the correct swing.

Perform a post-shot routine to reestablish tempo and regain momentum. It is your chance to get present-centered and back into the flow of your round. Practice your post-shot routine consistently on the range. You'll be surprised at how quickly you learn to move on from mistakes and get your mojo back.

Coach's Note: Never attempt to fix your swing when you play. Make adjustments. Use self-awareness to adjust your aim, your strategy, or your execution. Use the four R's – Responsibility, Review, Replace, Rehearse – to manage the duration, intensity or direction of your reactions to the results. Save your fixes for practice time on the range.

Reinforce: But don't forget good shots too! When you make a great shot we recommend immediately repeating the same motion to *reinforce* the movement, or the feel of a tension-free release, or mental skills that kept you focused. Reinforcing the swing allows you to recapture the feel and tempo of good shots, and to reinforce your thought process. After all, we are trying to find out what works and then repeat it. Why not repeat the great swings? Enjoy the good swings and let them sink in.

- When the shot matches your intention, identify actions, thoughts and emotions that facilitated performance, so they can be repeated and integrated into your pre-shot routine during practice sessions.
- When shots fall below your expectations, check your execution first. Did your Lock and Load steps set you up in your best position for success? Or did something in your thought process

or emotional landscape change to cause interference with movement?
- Note any changes in rhythm or tension. A break in the flow of setting up to the ball and swinging often indicates conscious or emotional disruption
- After your analysis, make either adjusting or reinforcing swings as a way to process the shot
- Use a process like the 4 Rs of Recovery to let go of the immediate shot and begin focusing on the next shot

Hold your finish position to process the results, because that is when learning takes place. Then make either an adjusting or reinforcing swing. It is a simple post-shot process, but if applied diligently it will greatly accelerate your learning curve. It will also help keep the wheels from falling off when you play. Holding your finish to learn and adjust or reinforce is the last step in your ultimate clutch routine.

Hold Checklist

- Hold finish position
- Suspend judgment
- Acceptance
- Internal feedback
- Rehearse
- Refocus
- Positive self-talk
- Describe your shot
- Anchor best swings

****

Develop Your Own Routine

We encourage you to use the Clutch Formula to develop your own ultimate pre-shot routine. We've included a fill-in-the-blank template in the Resources section to help you create one. It will help you decide which performance skills to include during specific steps and at specific times throughout your routine

Clutch Formula TEMPLATE

Step 1: Review the words below. Circle four words at each step that represent the highest priority skills or techniques to include in your routine.

LOCK	LOAD	FIRE	HOLD
• Analyze situation	• Action Cue (word, phrase or action):	• Remain focused	• Hold finish
• Pick specific target	• *Stay in rhythm*	• Stay committed	• *Suspend judgment*
• *Imagine shot shape*	• Set Up to ball	• Retain the target	• Acceptance
• Visualize trajectory	• *Take precise aim*	• *Swing in rhythm*	• *Feel Impact*
• Select Strategy	• Center mind	• Maintain trust	• Rehearse
• Pick club	• Center body	• Execute	• *4r's to Refocus*
• Narrow Focus	• Athletically ready	• Finish tall	• Positive self-talk
• Be intentional	• Focus	• Finish in balance	• Describe shot
• *Commit*	• Intention	• *Feel the swing*	• *Anchor*
• *Rehearse Feel*	• *Retain image*	• *Align body and mind*	• Adjusting swing
• Target Location	• Commit	• Free release	• Reinforcing swing
• Breathe	• Positive self-talk	• *Tension-Free*	• Finish
• Visualize	• *In sync*	• Release to target	• *Flow*
• Use Positive Self Talk	• Posture	• Connected	• Free
• Affirmations	• Center		
• Present-centered	• Breathe		
	• Waggle		

The Clutch Formula has the flexibility to incorporate any skill that helps you execute under pressure. Use the results from your Clutch Test to identify the skills to prioritize in practice and training. Incorporating performance skills into your pre-shot routine is the first step toward executing them during pivotal moments in competition.

Use the Formula to also improve your *proficiency* in those skills. Keep practicing each skill until it is automatic. Then stress-test it under pressure. Then learn from the results.

Introduce variability, variety and competition to encourage deep learning in long term memory. Include random and distributed drills that mimic on-course play to learn what it takes for *you* to hit clutch shots, with consistency, under pressure. Practice these skills as part of your routine.

Use the same routine on the course that you practice on the range. Practicing your routine on the range is the path to trusting your routine on the course. Always devote some portion of your practice time to transferring your range skills into playing skills.

But no matter how much you practice on the range, the true measure of your routine will come from playing. Learning to trust your routine when you play is a key to hitting more clutch shots more often. A well-practiced routine you can trust on the course is a bullet-proof way to either normalize the pressure or rise to the challenge, equipping you to hit the shot you need when you need it most.

Regardless of the techniques you use, the steps you take, or the order in which they occur, the elements of your routine should help you make smart strategy decisions, get mentally present, be physically centered, narrowly focused, and athletically ready. They should put you in position to swing with confidence.

When you play, pay attention to the effect a consistently executed routine has on your performance. We are confident you will notice a direct correlation between the quality of your routine and the quality of your shot.

Coach's Advice

1. Design a pre-shot routine that purposely enables you to be clear on your intention, focused solely on the shot at hand, and confident in your capabilities.
2. Write down your set-up routine, then practice it until your execution is automatic and your entire routine feels like a natural extension of your shot.
3. Keep it simple, like Kevin Sutherland, so you can just do what you always do.
4. Use action phrases like *Lock, Load, Fire* as prompts to execute your routine with consistency.
5. Practice like you play, where every shot means something and mistakes have consequences.

Chapter 7: The Clutch Formula In Action

Learning to perform well under pressure is developed through experience. Simulating pressure on the range is an effective way to prepare, but there is no substitute for facing real life situations and overcoming a meaningful challenge.

In this chapter we provide a series of exercises for both the range and on-course play. It's your opportunity to test your Clutch Formula skills and techniques in action. Read through the exercises, take them with you to the range and out on the course.

Concentrate at first on primarily observing. Look for trends and tendencies. Make notes. Keeping a journal or recording observations on your phone would be a great resource. Your observations will soon coalesce into priorities for game improvement and new skill development.

Brand Jobe provided an excellent account of the skills in action during hi Clutch Interview. His detailed descriptions of the thought process he used to choose a clear and specific strategy, the challenge of remaining focused despite being extremely nervous, and the techniques he used to maintain commitment to his shot are an inspiration. As was the confidence he developed in the way he prepared in advance for that shot.

Use the Jobe story – as well accounts from all the other Clutch Interviews – to create a personal yardstick to measure your own performance and execution skills under pressure.

Brandt Jobe's Major Decision

On the first playoff hole of sudden death, Brandt Jobe stood in the fairway with a decision to make: go for the par-5 green in two, or play safe?

At stake was a life-changing chance to win a major tournament: the 1998 Japan PGA Championship. Not only would winning one of Japan's two majors put a stamp on Jobe's fledgling career, it also carried a 10-year playing exemption. For a young Tour player, the security of not having to qualify every year meant everything.

Jobe's playoff opponent was Jumbo Ozaki, a national hero in Japan and the runaway crowd favorite. Ozaki, a seasoned veteran with over 100 worldwide victories, was playing the best golf of his career and had risen to the No. 2 spot in the World Golf Rankings. Jobe knew Ozaki was fiercely competitive and wouldn't hand him the tournament, particularly on his home turf. Jobe would have to beat him. Not only did he face an intimidating player, Jobe faced an equally intimidating 2nd shot. It's a scene he remembers vividly:

> *"Our first playoff hole was one of the most unbelievable par fives you've ever seen. The landing area was squeezed by water on the left and bunkers on the right. If you hit the fairway, then you faced a long second shot to an elevated three-tiered green. Not only did you have to carry water with a long club but the whole green was guarded by a 20-foot waterfall in front of it."*

Ozaki's tee shot ended up in the rough. Unable to go for the green, he would have to lay up. With the pin tucked in the back tier, Ozaki would have a difficult shot getting the ball close, making it a tough birdie but a likely par.

Jobe's drive, on the other hand, was in perfect position in the right center of the fairway. Jobe would have the advantage if he could hit the green in two. He'd have a putt for eagle. On the other hand, if his shot missed and hit the water, he would be practically handing the tournament to Ozaki.

Jobe faced a fierce opponent, a hostile crowd, a daunting 235-yard shot with a two-iron, over water, no margin for error, and a major title at stake along with the all-important 10-year exemption. All on the line. All on one shot.

> *"It was an overwhelming shot in every respect, and it was the most nervous I'd ever been in a tournament." Jobe told us. "Trying to hit a two-iron that far over water wouldn't have been something I would have done every time. But I thought it was my opportunity to beat him. And I took it."*

Intention is a pillar of clutch play. Jobe displayed it in spades. He knew the risks, but he also recognized the opportunity. In pivotal moments, intent must remain clear. Jobe was clear on the reasoning behind his strategy: he wanted to win, and he knew making the shot would give him an advantage. Clear intention kept his nervousness in check and gave him control over the situation. It enabled him to lock in to what he wanted to accomplish and to remain committed to that strategy.

> *"When I have a clutch shot in a situation where I know it's a big moment, I don't think about missing, or hitting a bad shot. I think about how I'm going to make it. Here's how I'm going to hit that putt. Here's how I'm going to hit that shot. There are no negative thoughts. Only the positives of what I'm going to do."*

Clear intention works hand-in-hand with focus when locking in to the shot. Jobe describes himself as a visual player, and he uses his ability to imagine the shot as one technique to narrow his focus.

> *"I'm a very visual player. When I get a very good visual picture of what I'm going to do, I'm successful more often than not."*

But for Jobe, visualizing is only the first step. He also locks in to what he feels. Getting a feel for the shot keeps focus in the moment, because feel only happens in the present. Feel is the critical connection between the Thinking and Athletic minds.

> *"It's such a game of feel." said Jobe. "I'm trying to get my body working in sync with what I'm seeing. When I get it and I go with that feeling, it almost always comes off."*

Feel for the shot comes in many ways. For Jobe it starts with what he sees in his mind's eye. Then the feel comes from his feet and the ground as he walks up. That feeling tells him what shot to hit. It's what he has learned works best for him. Jobe believes learning what works best is a critical part of evolving into a better player.

> *"I think that's what amateurs have to figure out: when you stand up to a shot, what do you feel? What do you see? What is that shot telling you? And whatever that shot's telling you, that's the shot your body wants to hit. That's the one you'll be most comfortable with."*

When you see it, feel it, and commit to it, you are locked in. And that's exactly how Jobe described the shot he hit:

> *"That's what part of a clutch shot is: it's a feeling that you get, that tells you* this *is the shot to hit," said Jobe. "I saw the shot, I felt the shot, and I got up and I hit the shot. Exactly what I saw and felt."*

It worked. Jobe's two-iron sailed over the waterfall, landed on the bottom tier of the green and jumped up to the second tier, leaving him a 25-foot putt for eagle.

> *"It was a 10 out of 10 at the time," said Jobe. "When all you think about is what you're trying to do, you get so focused on what's going to happen – not what could happen – that you pull off unbelievable shots."*

But Jobe knows he's not going to lock in if it's a shot he can't hit or hasn't practiced. Jobe was ready for the moment because he prepared for it.

> *"That week I knew I was going to be hitting a three-wood, two-iron, or three-iron into that hole. So I practiced it. I hit those shots on the driving range. In my mind I was on the course, hitting that shot as if it were the real thing. I knew my feels. I had prepared myself to hit that golf shot before I've even had it."*

Hitting a 235-yard two-iron under any circumstances is a challenge. Add in the pressure of a sudden death playoff for a Major championship and it requires absolute trust. Jobe trusted that he could hit the shot that would put him in position.

> *"I feel a clutch shot is really a shot that you've prepared to play for. So when you get to that moment and you've got to hit that shot, you've hit it so many times on the driving range that you know what it's going to do."*

Confidence came from his preparation, leaving no doubt in Jobe's mind. Confidence enabled him to maintain his focus and commitment throughout the shot.

> *"I stood over the shot and there was never, ever any thought of what could go wrong. The whole thought was what I was going to do. I got in some sort of a moment. A feeling where I didn't worry about consequences. Only what I was going to do," said Jobe. "You have the shot that you've hit on the driving range. One you've performed correctly. And all of sudden it's easy."*

Ozaki missed his birdie putt and settled for par. Jobe two-putted for an easy birdie and his first Major championship.

Jobe's advice for amateurs:

> *"Hit the shots that you know that you can hit, and that you've hit before," he says. "Clutch is going out there and knowing that you can hit the shot and then hitting it. You have to play within your abilities of what you can and can't do. It may not be the prettiest shot in the world: it may roll up on the green, it may slice, it may hook. But the ultimate goal is getting it from point A to point B."*

He also offers a caution:

> *"Amateurs don't hit enough shots that they've trained for on the driving range. They try and hit shots that they can't hit, and they're not going to be comfortable with hitting that shot. Clutch moments happen throughout the round. When people try to do things they can't do, they don't have as many clutch shots in the round, and they don't score as well."*

As the analysis of Jobe's clutch shot indicates, he made use of all four clutch pillars: deliberate practice, trust, focus, and intention. He did it through a process that included locking into the shot, loading the feel of the swing, and firing with total commitment.

Clutch Exercises

It takes time to reach a high skill level like Brandt's. Long-lasting improvement in your game isn't going to happen overnight.

But there is a path to follow.

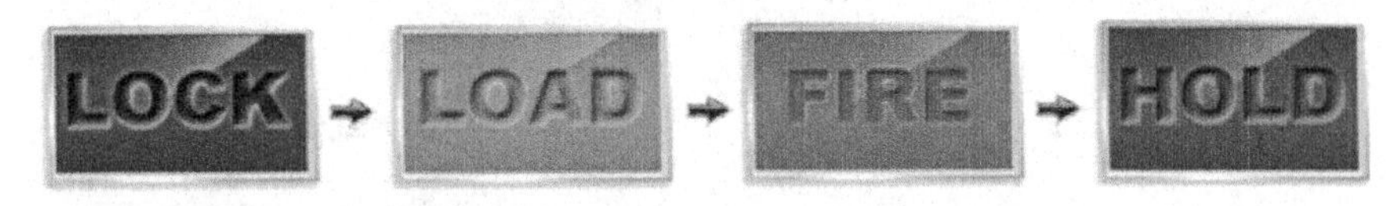

The remainder of this chapter provides a variety of exercises to get you started. Start small. Develop your skills with the long term in mind. As the proverb says *"The best time to plant a tree is 20 years ago. The second best time to plant a tree is today."* The best time to begin improving your playing skills is today.

The first exercise is to develop a pre-shot routine that includes your strongest and highest-priority playing skills. Design your initial routine to take advantage of best skills in order to build a strong core. Then expand in incremental steps.

Include just one skill at a time that addresses your weakest performance skills. Resist the temptation to try to fix everything at once.

Once you have created, practiced and tested your initial routine, use that routine for the remainder of the exercises. When a particular exercise improves your execution, modify your routine to include it in the process.

Don't fear! Everyone can do it. Small steps taken continually will deliver long lasting results. As Ben Hogan said:

> *"The best way to learn golf is a great deal like learning to play the piano. You practice a few things daily, you arrive at a solid foundation, and then you go on to practice a few more advanced things daily, continually increasing your skills."*

Here's your first exercise: The Clutch Formula Template

CLUTCH Exercise #1: Formula Template

The first exercise we recommend is to fill out the Clutch Formula template and create a pre-shot routine. The Template can be downloaded free at www.igolfu.com/course/clutch-resources

The template contains a laundry list of action words and techniques categorized under each of the Formula's four steps: Lock, Load, Fire, Hold.

Clutch Formula TEMPLATE

Step 1: Review the words below. Circle four words at each step that represent the highest priority skills or techniques to include in your routine.			
LOCK	LOAD	FIRE	HOLD
• Analyze situation	• Action Cue (word, phrase or action):	• Remain focused	• Hold finish
• Pick specific target	• *Stay in rhythm*	• Stay committed	• *Suspend judgment*
• *Imagine shot shape*	• Set Up to ball	• Retain the target	• Acceptance
• Visualize trajectory	• *Take precise aim*	• *Swing in rhythm*	• *Feel Impact*
• Select Strategy	• Center mind	• Maintain trust	• Rehearse
• Pick club	• Center body	• Execute	• *4r's to Refocus*
• Narrow Focus	• Athletically ready	• Finish tall	• Positive self-talk
• Be intentional	• Focus	• Finish in balance	• Describe shot
• *Commit*	• Intention	• *Feel the swing*	• *Anchor*
• *Rehearse Feel*	• *Retain image*	• *Align body and mind*	• Adjusting swing
• Target Location	• Commit	• Free release	• Reinforcing swing
• Breathe	• Positive self-talk	• *Tension-Free*	• Finish
• Visualize	• *In sync*	• Release to target	• *Flow*
• Use Positive Self Talk	• Posture	• Connected	• Free
• Affirmations	• Center		
• Present-centered	• Breathe		
	• Waggle		

Follow the template instructions to select key skills to include at each step, rank them in priority, and then condense them to an action phrase.

If this is your first pre-shot routine, choose words that represent areas of strength. The Clutch Test will be helpful in identifying the right skills. Building a core routine based on skills you are already good at will make the routine effective right from the start.

Practice your action phrase on the range. Use deliberate practice to focus on developing proficiency at specific skills and techniques within the action phrase.

Use your new routine on the course. Evaluate your routine by observing results. Refine your routine by adding or changing skills and techniques as needed.

Repeat the process several times each season, or whenever you feel your game could use a fresh approach.

****

The next series of exercises address each of the steps in the Clutch Formula, starting with the first step: Lock.

LOCK Exercise #1: Monitor Internal Dialog

If we could eavesdrop on the internal conversation of a clutch player during the LOCK step it might sound something like ...

"Ok. My drive ended up in the right rough leaving me a 7-iron distance to the green. Pin's in the middle but there's a tree between me and green. The rough isn't too long and the ball is sitting up so the lie is ok, but the grass is wet and could produce a flyer. I could hit a hard-7 over the tree or fade a soft-6 around it. There's no trouble left of the green, but plenty of trouble long and right, so I can't miss there.

I've got a one-shot lead on the last hole. This is a big moment because my opponent is in perfect position in the middle of the fairway. I have to protect my lead and put myself in position to salvage par or at worst bogey.

If I go with the hard-7 I'd be worried about getting it high enough to go over the tree and still reach the green. Hitting the tree might bring double-bogey or worse into play. I think I'll have better odds with the soft 6. I'm more comfortable with a fade and even if I don't make the green I'll still be in good position to get up and down, so that's the strategy.

Now the question is how much curve to put on it. Let's take a few rehearsal swings to get a feel and to figure out my starting line.

As I take a big breath my focus narrows until I can "see" my shot curving around the tree and landing on the green below the hole. Now I can start making rehearsal swings until what I feel syncs up with what I'm seeing: After a few rehearsals the swing that makes me most comfortable is to put a little more curve on it so I can aim farther away from the tree with a safer start line.

Now that I have my shot and starting line, I remind myself that I've hit this shot before in practice so I know I can do it again. I can clearly see what I want to do, I know where my target is, and have a good feel for the swing. It's a shot I can commit to. I'm locked in. I'm ready to step in and hit it."

Internal Dialog Exercise Analysis: If we trace the steps in this internal conversation, we see that our imaginary golfer followed a thoughtful and consistent process, using a number of mental skills – all in the space of 12 to 18 seconds. This is what he did:

- First followed a standard process to evaluate the lie, yardage, conditions and situation in order to arrive at a definitive strategy – the soft 6 fade
- Showed high situational awareness by acknowledging the pressure of the situation and risk/reward options
- Engaged self-awareness to recognize the potential concern he'd have trying to hit 7-iron over the tree
- Chose comfort – one of the three C's – to pick a safer shot strategy that would facilitate his confidence and was a shot he had practiced
- Used a breathing technique to narrow his focus to the present moment and shot
- Purposefully used visualization to engage the creative side of his Thinking mind in preparation to communicate with the Athletic mind

- Engaged his Athletic mind through movement, relaxation breathing and swinging
- Used rehearsal swings to synchronize the feel of the swing with the shot he visualized
- Identified a clear and specific target below the hole and retained that image through impact
- Used positive self-talk to bolster internal confidence and to manage his emotional landscape

There's a lot going on in the Lock step, yet it is all-too-often rushed, or ignored completely. Your exercise is to monitor your entire thought process the next time you face a challenging shot. Ask yourself these questions:

- Have you considered all the relevant factors?
- Do you have situational awareness?
- Do you take your realistic capabilities into consideration?
- Do you have a specific target?
- Can you clearly see and feel the shot in advance?
- Do you choose a strategy that makes you confident, and reinforce it with positive self-talk?
- Do you use performance techniques to assist execution?
- Do you follow a process to execute?

This is an internal awareness exercise. The goal is to develop awareness of your internal dialog as it is happening. Like meta-awareness or mindfulness, it is having an overall awareness of what is happening even while you are in the process of carrying it out. Once you have an awareness of the dialog you engage in to make decisions, you can control the content and direct of your thoughts.

The next exercise is designed to focus your attention at a specific performance skill: determining a clear strategy

****

LOCK Exercise #2: Strategy Clarity

This exercise will provide you with some interesting insights that may change the way you prepare to hit each shot.

The next time you play, keep track of the number of times you were 100% crystal clear on your strategy before you hit the shot. Do you know exactly what you wanted to accomplish and how you were going to go about achieving it? Did you identify a specific target? Visualize the shot shape and trajectory? Pick a shot that is within your capabilities?

Give yourself a 1 if you were clear and a 0 if you were not, or if you didn't even have a strategy. Keep a scorecard to track your strategy clarity. Your clarity score should match the number of shots you hit during your round.

Most of our students are shocked to learn how often they hit a shot without even having a strategy. Even the strategy they do pick is often more vague than they realize, with not enough target and shot specificity, and too much guessing and winging it. Try to hit it straight and hope for the best leaves the door open for too much interpretation and second-guessing.

After doing the exercise for just a few rounds you will find yourself almost automatically beginning to think through your shots more thoroughly before stepping in. The mere act of paying attention to your strategy will help you get better clarity more often, without even trying.

When you reach this stage, up the ante by grading the clarity of your strategy, as well as your ability to maintain total clarity through impact. Use a subjective scale of 1 to 10, counting only shots where your grade is seven or higher.

For example, hitting the fairway is a good intention, but it's too vague to pass the clear strategy threshold.

Fading it to the dark green patch of grass to the right of center, in line with the leaning tree on the horizon is a clear and specific strategy that would pass with flying colors. Effective strategies are clear, specific, and easy to visualize. They include the target, shot, and intention.

With better clarity and a firmer commitment to your strategy, you will quickly begin to see better, more consistent golf shots.

****

The next exercise is to time your set-up routine. Begin the moment you sole your club behind the ball, and end at impact. The goal is to execute within a consistent time frame, no matter the situation or circumstances.

LOAD Exercise: Time Your Set-Up Routine

The purpose of every set-up routine is to consistently get into the best physical and mental position to be successful. Repeat the same steps in the same order with the same rhythm until they are automatic. Use your set-up routine on every shot.

During a practice round at the AT&T ProAm at Pebble Beach, we had an opportunity to time the set-up routine for one of the best Pros in the world. He took 8.5 seconds from the time he soled his club behind the ball to the moment of impact. Over the course of nine holes he never varied by more than half a second. Same steps, same order, same rhythm every time, like a machine, and the results spoke for themselves.

Inspired by that example, we timed one of our college-bound juniors. Although he was an accomplished player with multiple wins, his play had become inconsistent. When we set up a session to time his routine, we observed an astonishing transformation.

The inconsistency showed up immediately in his set-up

routine, which varied from six to 11 seconds. After experimentation we reorganized his set-up steps and streamlined his routine. Then we shifted to repetition mode.

Within a handful of repetitions he stabilized at about eight seconds. What was even more enlightening was that he could also sense where he had been losing his focus and what was causing the interference in his prior routine.

After another handful of repetitions he was nailing the eight-second mark consistently within a half-second. His shot-making quality improved markedly. He reported that tuning in to his awareness of how time was flowing enabled him to sense the rhythm of the routine. Focusing on rhythm blocked everything out and produced a zone-like sensation of just being in the flow. The more he stayed in rhythm, the better his shots.

Your exercise is to have a friend time your Set-up Routine. Measure from the moment you sole the club to the moment of impact. See how consistent it is.

Find a perfect rhythm that is comfortable, and that allows you to accomplish everything you need to do. Then practice repeating your set-up routine. Set a goal to execute within half a second plus or minus either way. Rhythm is a powerful tool to combat the pressure of clutch situations.

Use the timing exercise on the range first to establish a comfortable rhythm for your set-up routine. Once you have a feel for how long your routine should be, observe how long it is actually taking when you play. Then observe if it changes in pressure situations.

****

The next exercise is the Target Description test. The goal is to combine a performance technique – visualization – with your descriptive skills to retain the target image more solidly in short term memory.

FIRE Exercise: Target Description Test

How clearly do you still see the target in your mind's eye at impact? Try this simple exercise of describing features to improve your target retention.

Look at the target from behind the ball. Pick a feature – any feature – and describe it to yourself. If your target is the pin, what color is the flag? Which way is the flag hanging? How tall is the flagstick? Which side of the green is it closest to? If your target is a tree on the horizon, what stands out about it? Any unusual shape or color? What about the trunk, limbs, or gaps in the foliage?

Once you have described a feature look away.

How much more clearly does the target image stay with you? How much better is your sense of the target location?

Hit your shot with the target description clearly in mind.

How well did you retain the target through impact?

The simple act of describing a feature provides a level of detail that creates a more realistic and complete picture of the target in your mind. The more detailed the image, the more clarity your Athletic mind will have about where the ball is supposed to go. Detailed descriptions make is easier to retain the target image all the way through impact. You'll release with more freedom and your accuracy will improve.

****

The next exercise is a spin on the set-up timing exercise described earlier. The goal this time, though, is to develop your self-awareness skills. As your self-awareness skills improve, it becomes easier to identify two of the major causes of non-swing mistakes: interference or process breakdowns (like Speith's missed step in his routine).

FIRE Exercise (Case Study): PGA Tour Rookie's Hesitation

Once your routine is set, you have a natural baseline from which variations can be observed. Dr. Glen and Eric experienced firsthand how inconsistencies in routines can reveal underlying issues that might otherwise never have been spotted.

While working with a PGA Tour rookie during a practice round, we observed our young Pro hit many quality golf shots. But we also observed him make a number of unforced errors.

Eventually we spotted a pattern: his set-up routine on quality shots was different than his set-up routine on mistakes. On good shots he took about eight seconds for his set-up routine, from the moment he grounded his club behind the ball to impact. On mistakes he took about 11 seconds.

That variation allowed us to discover that on the bad shots he hadn't fully made up his mind about what he was going to do. He was still deciding while he was addressing the ball.

The extra three seconds over the ball was allowing interference of all kinds to sneak in and affect his focus and commitment. As a result, it changed his rhythm and the way he released his club through impact.

To address it, we asked him to fully describe to his caddy the shot he intended to hit for every shot the remainder of the round. That description included the target, the trajectory and the shape of the shot. It also included the club he would use, along with the way he would change impact to get the ball flight he wanted. Shots to the green included a description of how the ball would land and roll out, and where it would finish.

Describing the detailed shot out loud forced our young Pro to have clarity about what he intended to do before he stepped in. The uncertainty cleared up and he played beautifully the rest of the way in. It was a telling example of how a consistent routine can provide a benchmark for evaluating performance, and why faulty technique should not automatically be blamed as the culprit of errant shots.

This exercise differs from the timing exercise in that the purpose is to discover underlying interference or process breakdowns that change the rhythm of the shot. Your objective is to be aware of any change in the timing of your set-up routine. If there is a change, evaluate your inner landscape and identify any causes of interference. Correcting the mistake is done not by fixing the swing, but by fixing the execution.

****

The next exercise focuses on mental skills: directing your thoughts to eliminate negative reactions by suspending judgment. Immediately after impact, you'll have your best opportunity to learn from the results. Conduct a post-shot routine to monitor your reactions. Once you have developed some skill in suspending judgment, you'll find it easier to make adjustments in real time on the course.

HOLD Exercise #1: Suspending Judgment

Thelonius Monk said: "The piano ain't got no wrong notes."

Avoid judging shots. Judgment creates an uncrossable gap between expectations and reality by attaching an emotional component to the outcome that you can't fix. You can't fix "bad," at least not the same way you can fix a shot that sliced high right because of an open club face. Negative judgments come with words like bad, horrible, or any of the many derivatives (awful, poor, suck, terrible, etc.). Emotional judgment clouds your reasoning, inhibiting your ability to process information in useful ways. Constantly judging shots makes for a long day on the course.

This exercise has two parts: one on the range and one on the course. The objective is to monitor your thoughts after each shot, counting how often you assign a negative judgment to the results of a shot.

Range Judgment Exercise

Hit a 10-ball set of shots to a target. In your post-shot routine after each shot, monitor your reactions for negative judgments. When you catch yourself judging, try instead to describe the outcome objectively: "It popped up and came down short."

Do not use negative judgmental words in your descriptions – just the facts.

Score yourself on how many times you were able to suspend negative judgments and reframe your analysis as an objective description.

Repeat the sets five times until you hit 50 balls. Average your suspending judgment score.

Course Judgment Exercise

On the course monitor your reaction after every shot. Add a "+1" to your score for every negatively judged shot. If you describe the shot objectively, or if you catch a negative thought and turn it into objective data, your score is zero. The result will be your "Judgment Handicap." Your goal is to become a Zero handicap at suspending judgment.

****

The next exercise is a structured post-shot routine. This process is particularly effective recovering from mishit shots.

HOLD Exercise #2: The Four Rs of Recovery

It is nearly impossible to stop the onset of emotional reactions certain shots, particularly mistakes. But there are three aspects of emotions you can manage. You can limit:

- ***Duration***
- ***Intensity***
- ***Direction***

One popular post-shot routine used to manage emotions is the Four Rs of Recovery. It is a structured process containing four steps. Use the 4 Rs to get your mojo back

Responsibility: *You hit it. Own the results. When you take responsibility for the shot, you can limit the duration of emotions by giving yourself a set time limit. Live with the emotions, then move on. Five or six seconds is enough for most golfers. Keeping duration short provides the opportunity to recover from the initial emotional intensity, and then to direct attention to the next shot.*

Review: *Analyze the results without judgment. It's just data: something you have to either adjust for, or note for skill improvement. Engage the Thinking mind in data analysis to reduce the emotional intensity and provide a different direction for your attention.*

Rehearse: *Take a few post-shot swings to immediately replace the feel of the errant shot with the feel of the correct motion and intention. Movement helps with both over-thinking and too much emotional intensity. Rehearsal swings allow the Athletic mind to reassert control, changing emotional direction and duration.*

Replace: *Replace mistakes with positive images of the correct motion and shot. Positive images can change the direction of emotions. Images help re-categorize emotions and channel them into productive intensity. Reframing a mishit as a new challenge also helps overcome the intensity of negative emotions, as well as shorten duration.*

****

As you build your pre-shot routine and work through the exercises, you will uncover many aspects of your performance that go well beyond swing technique. The good news is that what you discover will affect your playing skills, which will have far more impact on your scores than swing mechanics.

You will also discover which of your playing skills are strengths and which are weaknesses. As a result, you'll have a much more concrete idea of how to refine your routine and which skills to prioritize. All it takes is experimentation and an open mind.

Experimenting With The Clutch Formula

Everybody's pre-shot routine will be different. But all routines share similar characteristics and the same goal: to get yourself mentally focused and physically ready to hit the next shot.

There is no one "right" way to structure your routine. The right way is whatever process works for you. Only you have the insight into your game that tells you what to pick and choose, how to determine the steps, and the order they occur.

The major steps, though, provide an overall structure that remains relatively unchanged. Whether you use *lock, load, fire and hold* or any other action phrases like *see it, feel it*, or *think box, play box*, the action steps are a mantra designed to help you automatically bring forth specific behaviors and actions.

Pick an action phrase that can serve as a foundation, and build your routine around it. The most productive action phrases come from the player and match what they see, feel, or hear.

Use the Clutch Formula to bring your skills together within the action phrase. That action phrase can then serve as a framework for both learning on the range and for execution on the course.

- Once they are identified, clutch skills can be learned by deliberately focusing on them during practice
- Skills can be broken into components, which can then be systematically practiced and refined
- Mental techniques can be employed to enhance execution of performance skills at strategic points in the routine

- Execution skills can be systematically improved by training under simulated pressure or competitive stress situations that mirror on-course experience
- Baseline performance levels can be measured and tracked over time to verify progress and optimize practice priorities

Developing your own personal clutch formula will take experimentation and testing. Create a checklist of skills in your pre-shot routine to evaluate. Use subjective grading scales to create a system of comparison. Subjective scales help in the development of self-coaching and self-awareness skills. Grade performance skills during practice on the range to benchmark skill level and monitor progress. Then grade your execution when you play.

Plan on continuing to test and refine your routine until the day you hang up your sticks. Your routine will change incrementally as you discover tools and techniques that improve results. As you integrate them into your routine, you'll emphasize those specific aspects of your routine in practice until they can be executed automatically.

Once you have gone through the process of improving your skills at creating a clear strategy, you can use the same process for every other step of your routine.

If you've taken the Clutch Test, the results can provide a starting point to identify performance skills that need attention. Make a list of the ones you believe will help your game the most. After you've worked on them for a few months, take the Clutch Test again. See what's changed. We are confident that as your clutch test scores go up, your on-course scores will go down.

Organizing Your First Few Practices

There is no magic pill. If there were, someone would have already discovered it, and would be dispensing prescriptions by the millions.

What there is, though, is a magic approach:

- Identify specific performance skills
- Practice them on the range
- Try them on the course
- Refine them through deliberate training

Now that you know the concepts and the process, devote at least one entire range session solely to developing and testing your Clutch

Formula. Follow the same natural order you use to hit every golf shot to create your personal Formula:

- **Lock**: Experiment with different ways to lock in to your strategy, target, shot, and the feel of the swing that matches. Grade your focus and intention. The clearer your strategy, the better you'll lock into the shot.
- **Load**: Write down the major steps of your set-up routine. Practice them in the same order and at the same tempo and timing. Experiment with steps that get you mentally centered, focused in the present moment, and physically centered in your most athletic ready position. Time yourself. Grade yourself on the ability to repeat your set-up routine within half a second.
- **Fire**: Experiment with different ways to fire away without conscious control or emotional interference. Maintain your focus, intention, and trust. Grade your ability to release freely, without tension from interference.
- **Hold**: Use the few moments after each shot to conduct a post-shot routine. Hold your finish position, analyze the outcome, learn from the feedback, and then either reinforce or make adjustments. Grade your ability to suspend judgment and describe the results objectively.

The template included in the Resources section will help you identify the skills as you create your own Formula. Use the template checklist to work your way through the mental skills and techniques at each step of the Formula. Then use the templates to prioritize areas to emphasize for deliberate practice.

As you discover what works best for you, write down the steps of your own personal Formula in the order you use them to hit a shot. That will enable you to customize the Formula to fit your unique game.

Your Entire Game Will Improve

Although not every shot will be clutch, applying the Formula to every shot will improve your overall performance.

Focus, intention, and trust skills should be used for every shot, not just challenging situations. In fact, it will be advantageous to initially practice your pre-shot routine on normal or low-pressure shots to gain experience. Even on stock shots, you'll play with more clarity and confidence. You'll develop a level of trust that will enable you to execute at a high level – no matter how much is on the line.

Coach's Advice

1. Take action. Develop your clutch skills through deliberate practice, then test them on the golf course.
2. Create a pre-shot routine using the Clutch Formula Template. Practice it, test it, use it, and continually refine it.
3. Use the exercises to learn and develop specific skills. But also understand the process behind the exercises, so you can apply it to any skill or technique you choose to prioritize.
4. Organize your practice sessions by prioritizing near-term performance skills, but keep the long term game plan in mind.
5. Figure out what works best for you. Then improve your execution.

SECTION 4
CLUTCH GOLFER TOOLKITS

Chapter 8: Self-Coaching Toolkit

Since most amateurs don't have a professional coach providing regular feedback and guidance, the vast majority of your game improvement efforts will be up to you. The next best thing to having a coach would be having access to a knowledge base of coaching tools and techniques to help you self-coach.

The toolkits in the next few chapters are a compendium of models, tools, and methods used by top coaches. The more you know about what you are doing, why you are doing it, and how you should be doing it, the more effective you'll be at coaching yourself. The more tools you have, the easier it will be to design a structured approach to improving your game. The better the structure, the faster you'll improve.

One of the most valuable skills in your toolkit, as Conrad Ray's interview highlights, is self-coaching. His story of Maverick McNealy backing off a shot to have a conversation with himself is a lesson all golfers should take to heart: have the awareness to recognize when you need a reset.

Conrad Ray's Performance Coaching

Coaches see more than their share of clutch moments and clutch players. Every team begins the season with the goal of winning a championship. There are countless pivotal moments along the journey, and none as intense as when the top teams square up for the title. The battle to win it often comes down to who keeps it together the best under constant pressure. Helping players learn how to perform under pressure is one of their most important roles as a coach.

Stanford's Conrad Ray knows clutch from both sides: as a player and as a head coach. Ray played his college golf alongside Tiger Woods at Stanford, and was part of the team that captured the 1994 NCAA College Golf Championship. He won the NCAA Championship again in 2007, this time as Stanford's coach, earning him a spot on the very small list of elite golfers who've won an NCAA Championship title as a player and a coach. Ray's Stanford team captured the NCAA Championship again in 2019, earning him a second National Coach of the Year award. He's been inducted to the Northern California Golf Association Hall of Fame as well as the Golf Coaches Association of America Hall of Fame.

Stanford's underdog victory in the 2019 NCAA Championship was a testament to both the players and to Ray's approach to coaching for performance. They faced Texas, a program with a history of excellence that made match play for the sixth time in eight years, and finished runner-up in 2016. The Longhorns fielded a strong team that defeated Stanford in each of their three matchups during the 2019 regular season.

Stanford, though, was riding a hot streak. They closed the season with five consecutive victories and staged several come-from-behind victories in match play. In the championship round, Stanford fell behind early to Texas. But senior Isiah Salinda sparked a charge when he won four of five holes against the Longhorns' top player. Word spread, and coach Conrad sensed a surge of energy move throughout the team. The players responded, coming from behind to secure a 3-2 match play victory and the NCAA title.

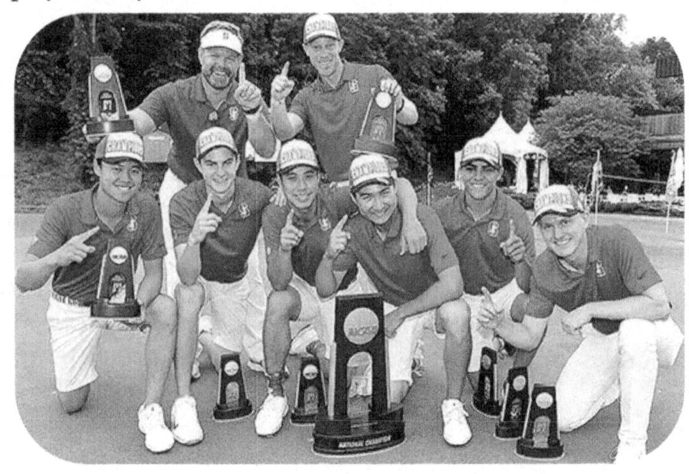

In his clutch interview, Coach Ray described one of the key skills players use to get themselves through tough spots: self-coaching. The players responded to pressure because they'd already practiced coaching themselves through so many challenging situations.

Ray provided an example of the value of self-coaching and the critical role it played in the career of one of his young players. That freshman went on to compile one of the best college records in Stanford history. But it wasn't Tiger Woods.

Tiger held many records at Stanford, that is until Maverick McNealy joined the team. McNealy won 11 college tournaments, tying Tiger's record, but bested Tiger's scoring average by more than half a stroke at 69.05. McNealy received the McCormack medal as the top-ranked amateur player in the world, and won the Haskins award as well as the Ben Hogan award for top collegiate player. But it was McNealy's clutch shot as a freshman that was the pivotal moment:

> *"Maverick was two over par and having a tough day when he got to the 8th hole at North Ranch. It was a 200-yard par-3 from an elevated tee to a firm and fast green, well-surrounded by bunkers and water. It was a very difficult shot. Maverick was in a mindset where, for the first time in his career, he didn't want to hit a shot. He felt like he didn't have enough confidence or the right frame of mind to actually be able to pull the club back."*

But then Maverick did something that showed his ability to not only recognize the situation for what it was, but also the ability to self-coach.

> *"What he did, though, after standing over it for a few seconds, was step off and have a conversation with himself. He reminded himself that being there was why he had worked so hard. That this was a moment he'd been looking for. He had the self-awareness to back off the shot, recollect himself, and refocus on what really needed to happen."*

Maverick stepped back into the shot, went through his routine, and hit it to two feet for a tap-in birdie. He proceeded to shoot five under on the back nine, and went on to collect his first collegiate victory.

Coach Ray believes great players understand that some situations mean more than others. But he notes that great players also have great self-awareness. It gives them the ability to conduct a positive self-dialogue, reminding themselves they've done this a million times, or that it's just a 7-iron and no more important than the three-footer they made on the first hole. They defuse the moment, and see it as it really is.

> *"Tiger, for instance, always talked about how he handled tough shots or important moments." said Coach Ray. "He would take a second and think about all the times he'd executed that type of shot over time, back when he was growing up or in his practice. He would consciously accept that he was nervous or that it was a big moment. But he reminded himself that it was still one shot, something he'd done a lot of times in practice, and that he was prepared to hit the shot. That's how he got in a frame of mind to execute efficiently."*

Coach Ray helps his players understand how to handle tough situations by learning to recognize important moments. Then he coaches them to avoid trying to play with blinders on. Instead, he wants his players to find ways to accept the situation, acknowledge the pressure, and then learn how to quickly get their mind to a state where they can execute. It takes focused practice and a willingness to experiment without fear of consequences.

> *"I think the tricky part is that you have to put yourself in those moments a number of times – and fail – to be able to learn and be self-aware," said coach Ray. "In the past, Maverick wouldn't have been able to back off, probably hit it in the lake, and then make a double bogey instead of a two-foot birdie. To evolve as a player, you have to experience things before you're able to execute."*

Developing this type of learned response – the ability to think and act positively under pressure – is something his players work on in nearly every practice. They practice hitting random variable shots, changing targets, shapes and clubs every time. They train with one-ball practice scenarios and simulated play. They practice situational shots. And they are constantly battling each other in challenges and competitions where there are consequences.

The goal is to recreate the pressure and feelings that come from being in challenging moments. Being able to execute the shot you need at the right time comes from practicing to play, not practicing to practice. Throughout these challenges, the players develop awareness of their responses, and then experiment to discover different response patterns that work better.

Developing a consistent routine is the glue that holds it all together. Coach Ray believes good routines start with the mental piece – getting clarity and the right mindset. He wants his players to answer three questions before they step into the shot:

1. *Are you clear on what a good shot looks like in this situation?* Are you able to strategically place your ball at a spot on the green, around the green, or off the tee that puts you in the best position to make the next one?
2. *Can you see that shot?* Is it something you've done or practiced before? Can you visualize it or feel how to make the shot?
3. *Does that work into a plan of action that fits your game?* Do you know your playing yardages or your slopes and do you have that shot?

When his players can answer those questions, they are ready to continue with their physical routine.

As Ray's example illustrates, high-level coaching emphasizes the development of high-level self-awareness. It starts with developing situational awareness and the ability to recognize the impact of key moments. Through the process of self-discovery, you'll discover your responses and then continually find techniques that help you respond even more effectively.

These awareness skills – situational awareness, self-awareness, and self-discovery – are the main components of your self-coaching toolkit. By applying these coaching skills with purpose, on a regular basis, you will significantly enhance your rate of progress and accomplishment.

The Power of Self-Coaching

Professional athletes spend years honing their athletic skills. During the process they develop, of necessity, high level self-coaching skills. It takes high-level self-coaching skills to reach the highest performance levels. Elite athletes make it look easy because they understand the *process* of applying feedback efficiently and discovering ever better ways to perform. They learn how to learn.

As one of the most valuable resources in your coaching toolkit, self-coaching is the key to becoming a clutch player. Nobody can do it for you, and information alone is not enough.

Self-coaching enables you to learn about yourself and then use what you learn to make meaningful, positive change. By deliberately seeking knowledge, cultivating skills, and implementing a process, you will continue to learn, make changes, and improve. You'll also remain motivated and will sustain effort over a longer period of time.

Self-Coaching Skills

Self-coaching requires a different set of skills than athletic playing skills. The coach's role is to provide guidance, direction, and accountability. They create the structure, playing an integral role as part of a team that is on a journey with a defined destination and objective. They plan the work, and let the athlete work the plan. Coaches motivate and encourage, all the while asking athletes to take responsibility for their efforts and outcomes. Coaches teach technique when appropriate, while keeping the goal of improving performance at the forefront.

When you self-coach, it's up to you to do all the things a coach would do.

Your skill at self-coaching will determine how far you can go and how fast you'll get there. Improving your skill at self-coaching will make practices fun and engaging and it will make your golf game a never-ending source of the wonder of self-discovery and the joy of achievement. As Michael Murphy wrote in *The Kingdom of Shivas Irons*:

> *"Golf is first a game for seeing and feeling. It demands a stillness of mind and sensitivity to all that is around you. Golf is a game for listening to the messages from within, and once you have paid attention it becomes a doorway to marvelous realms."*

Mastering the skill of self-coaching is a critical step toward performing at the highest level. It's the most important general purpose application in your toolkit because it influences the speed and efficacy with which you develop every other skill in your game.

Think Like A Coach

If you were a coach working with only one athlete – ***you*** – how would you coach yourself? What would it take for your athlete to reach their highest level of performance? What knowledge base and what tools would you use to coach them?

Self-coaching is much more than just watching where the ball goes. It's a systematic process for interpreting shot information, analyzing the feedback, and making adjustments. It is also suspending judgment, and using a system for self-diagnosis and self-correction.

Self-coaching is also the ability to see the big picture, break it down to specific objectives, develop an action plan, maintain motivation, track results, measure progress, and reach goals.

Self-Awareness Comes First

Self-awareness is the lynchpin of self-coaching. The greater the awareness of how you think, feel and react, the easier it will be to coach yourself to a higher level of performance. Becoming attuned to your senses enables you to develop a deeper feel for your swing, and provides a more sophisticated insight into your thought processes.

Quality practice and competition provide the experience to continually develop your awareness, provided you do it intentionally. The more refined your level of self-awareness, the more effective you'll be at self-coaching, and the better you'll play. As *Extraordinary Golf* author Fred Shoemaker said:

> *"I've seen an inverse relationship in golf: As your awareness grows your handicap shrinks. When a person's awareness grows, there's no possibility of them playing worse. They always play better."*

Focus, intention and trust – three pillars of clutch play – are all intangible skills. All three can be improved through self-coaching. These skills are sensed through internal feedback. They are subjective, and so are not directly observable. But with conscious attention, these critical skills can be learned and mastered.

Intentionally focusing on your reactions under pressure situations will activate your internal awareness system. The more self-awareness you develop about the way you think, feel and react, the easier it will be to proactively incorporate helpful performance skills.

Your Internal Feedback System

The source of feedback lies in your sensory systems. All movement, all thoughts, all the ways you experience things and the ways you interpret those experiences, along with the ways you respond, come through your internal sensory systems. When you hit a shot, you have access to a tremendous amount of information. Self-awareness is developed by tapping into your sensory and nervous systems to isolate and interpret specific feedback.

A well-developed internal feedback system for golfers involves the collaboration of all your senses: sight, sound, feel, smell, taste, thoughts and emotions. Selectively paying attention to specific feedback provides awareness of what happens to you physically, mentally, and emotionally under stress. Your sensory system includes:

- Kinesthetic and visual awareness of the target, the ball flight, and your own swing
- Athletic awareness of your body position, balance, swing dynamics and tempo
- Auditory pre-awareness of a well-struck shot or the sound of the ball falling into the cup
- Tactile awareness of the feel of the club as it strikes through the ball and pulls you into a well-balanced finish position
- Internal awareness of your thoughts and emotions before, during, and after the shot
- Physical awareness of involuntary reactions such as heart rate, breathing, muscle tension, perspiration, vision and others

Each of these feedback sources can be deliberately engaged during practice and while playing. Peak performance is built on this intrinsic feedback during the round. When players are "in tune" with what they see, feel and experience, their play is elevated. The better they play, the more in-sync they become. And the more in-sync they become, the better they play. It's a positive feedback loop that can lead to a flow state or to being in the Zone. But as with all other aspects of the game, it is critical to practice accessing your internal sensory system through self-discovery on the range first, in order to effectively self-coach yourself on the course.

Self-Discovery is the Action Plan

The primary tool used to enhance your self-awareness is the process of self-discovery.

Self-discovery occurs through creative experimentation, trial and error, adjusting, refining, and reflecting. Sometimes self-discovery is just playing around, exploring the boundaries of what you can do, and then pushing the limits. It combines action with observation. It's also about diving deep into your internal feedback system, and being in tune with your inner mental and emotional landscape, as well as your kinesthetic, visual, tactile, and auditory senses.

Self-discovery should be fun, interesting, challenging, frustrating, and ultimately rewarding. There are no rights or wrongs: only doing, testing, observing, and learning.

For instance, imagine you've set a goal to improve the number of fairways you hit per round. The action step could be to maintain a clearer target focus through impact. Using self-discovery techniques, you'll test multiple focusing techniques until you discover the one that works best. Through action and analysis, you'll discover the answers.

Self-discovery is a natural process we've all been perfecting since birth. It is the oldest and most referred motor learning theory: observe, imitate and experiment. Our minds are hard-wired to learn through self-discovery: We try, we fail, we adjust and try again until we get it. And if we stick with it, we always get it. After all, how do you think you learned to walk?

It takes time and repetition to develop internal awareness. New golfers have to "discover" what it feels like to hold a club correctly, make a swing, and hit the ball. They use a lot of trial and error. It also takes time for experienced golfers to discover how to make a swing change. They test different swings, feel the differences, and analyze the results. Then they have to discover how to repeat it under pressure.

Self-discovery can be applied to physical movements as well as mental skills or performance techniques. Through selective attention, you may catch yourself giving mental instructions, or focusing on mechanical swing thoughts. You may discover interference from fears, uh-ohs, oopsies or other mental chatter. When you are able to match your thoughts to changes in the feel of the swing, you gain the ability to discover what is truly influencing performance. Self-discovery will enable you to name the interference, and once you have a name for it, you can control it.

Great coaches direct the athlete's attention to the appropriate places so that discovery can occur. They draw feedback out of the athlete by asking questions such as: *How did that feel? What did you experience? What did you notice? What was the difference between what you wanted and what happened?*

Coaches also enable golfers to discover interference. To be a great self-coach, learn to ask yourself these same types of questions of yourself after a shot. The clutch routine template in the Resources section can be used as a resource by turning selected skills into questions. *Did I stay committed? Was I present-centered and task focused?* Use the process of self-discovery to enhance your self-awareness, and through that your ability to self-coach.

Quality Feedback is Key

The key to maximizing your performance potential is the nature and quality of your feedback. Coaches tailor the information and instruction to the student's skill level and learning style. You should too.

Whenever possible, use some form of objective measurement or metric for feedback. *Boy, I really let that one go and made great contact. That was a 10.* When objective feedback is not available, use subjective scales. *I had a little doubt about that shot and it interfered with my intention. I'm giving that one a 6.*

High quality feedback:

- Accelerates the trial-and-error phase
- Reduces the number of trials needed
- Eliminates guesswork through quantifiable results
- Provides a higher level of refinement and calibration
- Makes it easier and faster to change or adapt

Consulting guru Peter Drucker, often described as the founder of modern management practices, is credited with saying *"If you can't measure it you can't improve it."*

High quality feedback includes:

1. Observable Metrics: *How many drives out of 10 can I hit into a 25-yard wide fairway?*
2. Internal Senses: *How many tension-free swings can I make with a rating of eight or better in a 10-ball set?*

Both observable metrics and internal feedback are essential when conducting performance training and execution practice. They provide relevant, definitive feedback golfers need to make changes, develop new habits, and execute to their abilities. They also prevent golfers from sliding back toward old habits.

Be purposeful in structuring range time to include measurements. Metrics, whether internal or observable, are critical for creating a realistic picture of your game. Plus, we have observed time and again how deeply engaged golfers become when they challenge themselves to beat established performance levels. They get immediate, measured feedback that rewards effort and sustains motivation.

When students have to dig deep into their sensory systems to get answers for themselves, they become fully engaged. That's when self-discovery and self-awareness skills kick into high gear. Deep learning happens when golfers get in touch with the feel of their swing at a fundamental level. The more shots they hit and the more accurate feedback they get when fully engaged, the more refined their sense of feel becomes. And golf is ultimately a game of feel. As Dave Pelz said:

> *"Great golfers don't think, they just feel. The pros imagine the shot they want to hit, then their minds let their bodies do what their bodies already know how to do. The best players see what they want to do before they do it. They don't think about mechanics, they just feel the swing they want."*

Striving to reach ever higher performance levels is the essence of the mastery approach. Mastery is not about making a six-footer. It's about challenging yourself to master the skill of making six-footers. Deliberate practice is an essential component of the mastery approach, and accurate feedback is a key part of deliberate practice.

We want to caution you, though, that getting it wrong during the self-discovery process is not a bad thing.

It's Not About Getting It Right

Think you have to do it right every time?

Think failure is something that should be avoided at all costs?

Think again.

Thomas Watson built IBM into a mega-corporation by embracing failure:

> *"Would you like me to give you a formula for success? It's quite simple, really. Double your rate of failure. You're thinking of failure as the enemy of success. But it isn't at all. You can be discouraged by failure – or you can learn from it. So go ahead and make mistakes. Make all you can. Because, remember that's where you'll find success. On the far side."*

When in self-discovery mode, it is important to understand that the quality of the shot, or its proximity to the target, is not an indication of the success or failure of the shot. Becoming more aware is.

Learn to separate the outcome of the shot from the measurement of success. Avoid judging shots as good or bad. Remember that you are engaging in a discovery process, not a perfect-it process. When you are able to tell the difference between really happened compared to what you wanted to do, then your awareness has improved. The shot can be chalked up as a success.

Failure Must Be an Option

In self-discovery mode you should expect to fail. A lot. Particularly if you are working on a new skill or making significant swing changes. Failure is an integral part of the process. In fact, the faster you fail, the faster you will achieve success. Go for it! We give you permission. Fail spectacularly. Fail often. You'll fail your way straight to success.

We have unfortunately seen too many golf lessons and practice sessions when the student's focus is in the wrong place – getting the shot right. This is an *outcome* focus. Focusing on outcomes is an extremely frustrating experience because when the golfer is trying to make a swing change, they seldom hit good shots. It is understandable that we would rather perform a skill well, but mistakes are what drive learning.

If we never make mistakes, we would never develop. We would simply reinforce what we already do. It is only when things do not go according to plan that we are forced to rethink and to devise new strategies and approaches. Legendary UCLA basketball coach John Wooden said:

> *"If you're not making mistakes, then you're not doing anything. I'm positive that a doer makes mistakes. Learning necessarily involves errors and attempts to overcome them."*

Instead of measuring progress in terms of better results, technique-focused practice should be measured as an increase in self-awareness: the ability to distinguish between what you felt and what really happened. The appropriate time to focus on outcomes is during performance training (when you are measuring results), or during transfer training (when working on execution and hitting a shot to a target).

It is important to make progress. It's a lot more fun for the student to have a series of successes than it is for them to grind away trying to make a swing change, not knowing if it is working based solely on how the ball flies. It is just as important to reward small gains (perhaps more important!) than it is to reward reaching an outcome. The overall goal is reached through incremental step changes. Freeing yourself up to engage in self-discovery, without judgment or concern for mistakes, adds joy to your journey.

Consistency Comes From Automaticity

Effective practices are not always about experimentation, though. At some point in your trial-and-error process you'll figure out what works. When you hit a shot the way you want, it's time to stop experimenting, and focus instead on consistently reproducing the execution. Effective practices, therefore, budget time to transition from experimentation to performance and execution training.

Through performance training and execution practice you develop trust in your ability to repeat. With sufficient repetition, the execution becomes automatic. Whether it is a physical swing skill or a mental performance skill, automatic execution is the bedrock of consistent play.

When do you transition from experimentation to performance training?

There are a number of models in the next chapter that describe the stages of proficiency we experience when making changes or learning new skills. Understanding the models will help you understand when to transition by enabling you to:

1. Recognize the stage of motor learning you are in, in order to tailor the right feedback and set appropriate expectations
2. Measure progress so you can get to the next stage faster
3. Keep the goal in sight, which is to execute automatically

Good teachers are able to recognize which stage the student is in and tailor their information appropriately. As a self-coach you will need to be able to recognize the learning stage you are in, so you can coach yourself appropriately and select the right training activities.

Coach's Advice

1. Develop your self-coaching skills. They'll be your most valuable tools for improvement.

2. Use the core self-coaching skills of situational awareness, self-awareness and self-discovery in a structured approach to improve your playing and performance skills.

3. WARNING: Resist the temptation to fix your swing after mistakes. Getting it wrong isn't necessarily a bad thing. Don't fix the swing; fix the execution.

4. Improve consistency by practicing your entire pre-shot routine and swing until your actions are automatic. Develop automaticity by transitioning from experimentation to deliberate practice and execution training.

5. Adopt a mastery approach. Be a lifelong learner.

Chapter 9: Inner Skills Toolkits

There is no one right way to self-coach. Use as many tools and techniques as you can to refine your abilities and, as Coach John Dunning advises, find your style. This chapter provides several models that address the way you learn, execute, manage emotions, and play with confidence, starting with a brief overview of each model.

Motor Learning Models provide an understanding of the physical skill developmental process everybody goes through when acquiring new skills or making swing changes. Knowing where you are in the motor development process will help you plan out the right activities, at the right times, in your practice. More importantly, it will help keep you focused on the ultimate goal, which is to keep improving until the movement is automatic. It's all too easy to get stuck working in the technique stage when the real goal is to move to the execution stage where everything happens automatically.

The Three Minds concept developed by Dr. Albaugh provides a unique perspective into the way different parts of our brain specialize in managing the way we think, feel, and create movement. It puts into context which parts of the brain are best suited to develop strategy, which manage emotions, and where physical movement is controlled. The goal is to turn execution of the shot over to the Athletic mind, which controls movement. Knowing when to engage different areas of the brain – and when to disengage them – is critical to performing at your highest levels.

The Emotional Landscape provides a measurable context for the scope of emotions experienced when we play. Not all emotions are bad! There are as many positive emotions as negative. The Emotional Landscape is a simple way to categorize emotions and to identify your ideal emotional intensity state. Since emotions play such a major part in performing under pressure, the ability to manage them and to control their influence is a key performance skill.

Confidence Models describe the difference between internal and external confidence, and explain why building internal confidence is more reliable over the long term. The three Cs of Confidence model describes how choosing strategies based on comfort, concentration, and commitment.

Your self-coaching skills will evolve over time as your game evolves and as you discover new approaches and techniques. The key point, as Coach Dunning points out, is to meet the needs of the athlete where they are. Play to who you are, and under pressure, stay true to your style.

Coach John Dunning: They Danced and Sang

John Dunning is a coaching legend in the annals of Women's college volleyball. Inducted into the American Volleyball Coaches Hall-of-Fame, he won five NCAA Women's Volleyball Championships, was the Pac-12 Coach of the Year four times. His .828 career winning percentage puts him among the five winningest coaches of all time. He coached more Division 1 National Title matches than anyone in volleyball history, and in his 32 years coaching volleyball, he took his teams to the NCAA Tournament 32 straight times.

Coach Dunning, a former student of Dr. Albaugh, has been through more clutch moments and coached more clutch players than he can count. But as he told us in his clutch interview, his final year at Stanford and the team's run to the NCAA Championship is one of his most dramatic memories.

Stanford started the 2016 season ranked 13th. Half-way through the season their record stood at a disappointing 10-7. There were growing concerns about even *making* the NCAA tournament. At that point Dunning made a clutch coaching decision: he shuffled the lineup and started a freshman at the pivotal setter position. The team suddenly gelled, winning 16 of their last 17 matches.

When they reached the NCAA Championships, Stanford fought their way through the tournament brackets, staging several dramatic come-from-behind victories along the way. They made it to the finals, only to face the powerhouse Texas Longhorns. The Texas program was a perennial force in women's volleyball. They had sent teams to the Final Four in each of the five past seasons and eight of the prior nine. Stanford was the clear underdog.

> *"We were a very young team with four freshmen in the starting lineup. All the talk was 'you've never been here before. You're too young to win.'"*

But Dunning used youth to his advantage. Stanford was the Cinderella story of the tournament. There were no expectations. The team could be whoever they wanted to be. And that's when Dunning made another pivotal coaching decision:

> *"I used to be a relentless teacher of technique. I used to think that if we had better skills than everyone, we might just beat them," said Dunning. "But in this situation I decided to think more about the personality of this team."*

Great coaches evolve their coaching skills just as athletes evolve their playing skills. Your skill and proficiency at self-coaching will change as well. Dunning explained how his thinking changed:

> *"The important thing was to let them be who they were going to be. In critical moments it's about being true to your personality. I made a decision that was contrary to what I typically would do, because the personality of that team was to have fun. I let them pick music and a dance routine, and that's what they did before we went out to play the final match. They danced and sang. That's who they were, and they stayed true to that."*

The decision paid off. The team was in sync from the opening serve and handled key moments with devastating effectiveness. Stanford went on to upset Texas 3-1 and win the NCAA Championship.

For Coach Dunning it came down to developing trust. He believes the magic happens when the players learn who they are and how to trust themselves:

> *"You have to go through a process. Everyone – the greatest players, the middle players, the players that are the youngest or least developed – they have to build belief. They have to find a style that works for them, and*

then build a belief in themselves and their technique that is not shatterable. That grows. But it has to be true. It has to be real."

Getting athletes to the next level is a balance between technique and style. But sometimes that means the athlete needs a push, and that's the role of the coach.

> *"Coaches have to drive players," said Dunning. "Someone has to let them know that the bar has just been raised and then hold them accountable to take that next step up the rung to be a better player. I held them accountable when I needed to."*

It isn't easy. The motivation has to come from somewhere.

> *"People want to be comfortable. They like being where they are. But to be as good as you want to be, you have to get out of your comfort zone. It's hard. It's painful. It's like, 'I was good. Now I'm not as good and I don't like it.'"*

One principle, however, remains very clear to Dunning:

> *"You can't be as good as you want to be unless you face competition and moments that challenge you. You can't be clutch and handle difficult situations if you don't face them regularly."*

That's why Dunning employs such a broad coaching toolkit.

Sometimes it was holding athletes accountable to a higher standard, other times it was lending a supporting ear. Sometimes the focus was on technique, other times execution. Sometimes it was strategy, sometimes tactics. Sometimes it was competitive, sometimes it's just having fun. Some days they just danced. When it's true, it works.

> *"The thing that holds it all together is the day-to-day preparation. That's how we help them believe in themselves."*

When you know who you are, the situation doesn't dictate to you. You already know how you are going to respond regardless of the circumstances, because that's who you are. That's how you control the moment. The key skill, according to Dunning, is maintaining the clarity to make good decisions.

> *"The difference maker in key moments is decision making. Pressure, our reaction to our ourselves and to the world around us – they all are challenges to our decision-making ability. What percentage of shots are you in the moment, clearly looking at the situation, and making the highest level, the best decision you could make?"*

Dunning's coaching toolkit is vast after 32 years of coaching. It allows him to mix and match training activities whatever way he thinks will best help his players.

> *"The coach has to use everything at their disposal to get the players to believe in themselves," said Dunning. "Now I provide a framework that's educational. We try to raise our player's athletic IQ. You have to have a process for making decisions. You have to clearly analyze the situation, make a good decision, and then execute."*

It is a practice Dunning developed into an art form. To excel at coaching yourself, follow his advice to develop unshatterable trust. And then drive yourself to reach the next, higher bar.

Learning Models

Learning models help us understand the process and stages we go through to acquiring new skills. Breaking the process into stages – from beginner to expert – provides a framework for prioritizing activities and allocating time. Knowing what learning stage you are in will help you improve faster, manage practice and training time more effectively, and take control over your journey to better golf.

The key takeaway from the learning models is that there is a path that progresses from the first uncoordinated efforts of learning a new skill to the ultimate stage of executing without conscious thought. You *will* go through each stage. There are no shortcuts. But the model can help you do it efficiently.

Automaticity is the final stage of the motor learning models. Our best golf happens when learned skills become automatic. It is the end goal. Knowing where you are on the motor learning curve will help you set appropriate expectations, as well as pick appropriate activities for practice and training.

The Motor Learning Model

How did we learn to walk? Talk? Toss a ball? What is the process we go through when we learn a new movement? How do we start out as a complete novice and end up as experts?

Sport Psychologists and cognitive scientists have been studying the skill acquisition process for decades. They have identified a number of different stages that share common patterns and activities. One frequently cited model developed by Richard Schmidt, a legend in the motor learning world, is the Motor Learning Model. The model uses three stages to describe the skill progression, from brand new to highly precise movement.

1. **Cognitive Stage**
2. **Associative Stage**
3. **Autonomous Stage**

By understanding the stages of motor learning, you'll be able to track your progress on your motor learning curve. You'll also move through the stages faster by employing purposeful practice and training. The goal of the Motor Learning model is to reach the final stage – the Autonomous Stage – where you develop the ability to swing without conscious thought.

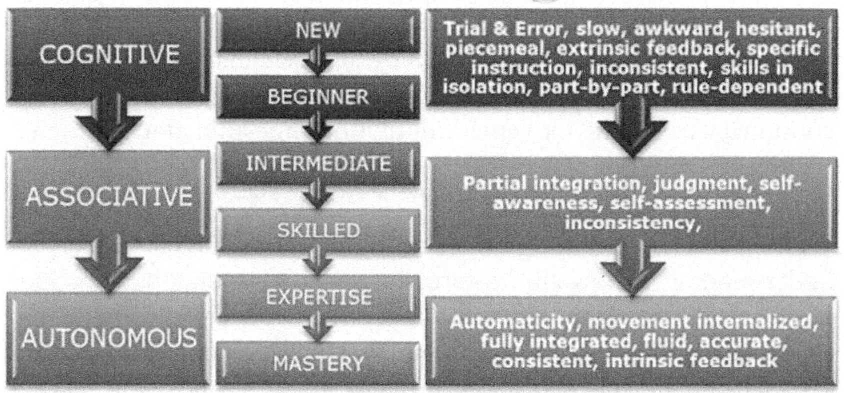

Motor Learning Stage 1: The Cognitive Stage

The beginning stage of the motor learning process is the Cognitive phase, because much of the activity during this stage takes place in the Thinking part of our brain. The primary goal is simply to grasp the concept of what to do. Because the physical movement is new and awkward, we expend considerable mental energy attempting to compile a detailed internal representation of each individual aspect of the movement, as well as the sequencing. Every little part of the movement has to be dissected and understood before it can be linked up to every other little part of the movement.

The grip, for example, is second-nature to a seasoned golfer. But for a brand new golfer, it is far more complicated. Beginners have to think about which hand goes on top, how the club is supposed to rest in the hands, where the thumbs go, whether to interlock, overlap, or use a 10 finger grip, how tightly to hold on, and more.

During the Cognitive stage we engage in significant internal dialog. We give ourselves verbal instructions as we experiment and think about alternative ways to accomplish the tasks. We rely on feedback from a teacher, the flight of the ball, and the feel of the clubface at impact. There is considerable trial and error experimentation as we attempt to grasp every detail and control every movement.

As a result, the swing is often jerky, hesitant and forced. Results during the cognitive stage are at the lowest level of the performance pyramid, characterized by significant inaccuracy and inconsistency.

The quickest way to move through the cognitive phase is to use deliberate practice techniques and keep expectations at a minimum. Focus on the process of self-coaching and celebrate small gains. Use trial-and-error and the Goldilocks approach, without judgment, to continually refine the movement until it becomes functional.

Motor Learning Stage 2: The Associative Stage

With sufficient time and repetition, the athlete gains an understanding of how all the parts link up in a continuous movement sequence. They have entered the Associative Stage, where each individual part of the movement becomes "associated" with a broader movement pattern. Grip, alignment, stance and posture becomes *set-up*. There will be an improvement in results, although performance will not be accurate or consistent.

Coach's Note: One efficient way to advance through the associative stage is to *borrow* from other sports movements and "associate" them with golf. Athletes who reach a high competency in one sport often find that similar movement patterns apply to both.

For instance, a tennis player may discover that their cross-court return stroke employs many of the same movements as a golf swing. Getting the tennis racquet into position, shifting weight, rotating, bringing the racquet into the impact zone, hitting the ball and following through mimics the golf swing sequence. The tennis player doesn't have to re-learn those movements. They "borrow" from their tennis movement and adapt it to their golf swing. They *associate* previously well-learned movements from one sport and apply them to golf.

Making a swing change typically involves spending some time in the Cognitive state, followed by a significant amount of time in the Associative phase. You already know how to make the larger overall movement, so the focus must be isolated on just one particular aspect of that movement.

The hinge, for example, is just one part of a larger movement pattern: the backswing. But determining when to hinge and how much to hinge requires specific focus during the learning stage. While you are figuring it out, the shots will be erratic. Eventually the isolated movement has to be integrated into the larger movement sequence. Until the movement graduates to the automatic stage, the results will continue to be inconsistent.

It is easy to get stuck in the Associative phase. Golfers who don't know better constantly tinker with their mechanics. They endlessly loop from one stage 2 activity to another. It keeps their level of play lower than it should be. Unless new swing changes are put through performance training and execution drills, the golfer will have a difficult time advancing to the next higher level of performance.

Coach's Note: Keep in mind that if you are working on a swing change, *it is for the swing of the future.* The swing you have now is the one you have to score with. Maximize results with the swing you have now by including performance training and execution drills along with your technique work. There is room in every golfer's practice schedule.

Motor Learning Stage 3: The Autonomous Stage

Ultimately we reach the third stage of Motor Learning: the Autonomous stage, where movement is automatic. Like walking and talking, the movement requires very little conscious thought. Automatically executed movements are precise, accurate, and economical. They are fluid, rhythmic and consistent.

Autonomous movement is developed through repetitive practice and performance training. It is refined through execution drills designed to minimize cognitive involvement and maximize automatic movement. Automaticity plays a key role in performing at a peak level, particularly under pressure.

The Motor Learning models provide an understanding of the path to automatic play, allowing us to expedite our progression to the highest levels of performance.

Pick the skills that provide the biggest payoff and work through the stages until you reach automaticity. The trust drills described by Dr. Albaugh in *Winning the Battle Within*, for instance, are designed to facilitate progress to the automatic stage, where conscious thought is not involved. The drills help golfers tap into their sensory feedback while turning off thoughts and balancing emotions, allowing golfers to swing without interference.

Coach's Note: Keep in mind that these models are skill specific. They don't reflect the state of your entire golf game. Different parts of your game will be at different skill levels and different stages of the development process at any given point in time. Your practice session activities should change accordingly.

The Three Minds of Performance Model

In the late 1990s, Dr. Albaugh combined ideas from eastern philosophy with contemporary thought arising from the human potential movement to create a performance model for golfers. The *Three Minds of Performance* model provides a framework to understand how different parts of our brain create thoughts, emotions, and actions to influence the way we play. Based also on biology, the model considers the role of evolution selecting different parts of our brain to specialize in distinctly different activities:

- **Thinking Mind**: The newest part of our brain – the neocortex and prefrontal cortex – specializes in higher-order thoughts, ideas, images and language
- **Emotional Mind**: A different area of the brain – the limbic area and amygdala – is the home of emotions
- **Athletic Mind**: The oldest areas of the brain – the motor-cortex and cerebellum, or reptile brain – controls movement and sensory feedback.

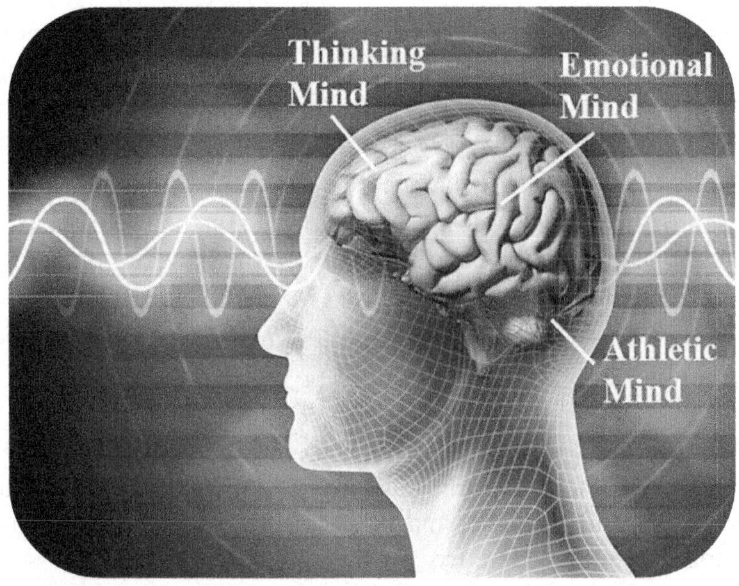

Although the brain is considerably more complex, the model nonetheless provides a simple framework with a practical application for golf.

Each specialized area of the brain carries out a variety of tasks at different times for specific outcomes. The specialized minds are very good at what they do, but terrible at everything else. As long as they stick to what they do best, and don't interfere with the other specialization areas, the golf swing goes off without a hitch.

For instance, voluntary movements like the golf swing begin as an idea in the Thinking mind. There is always a guiding thought to what you want to do, before you actually do it. But the Thinking mind does not directly control movement. It has to send the guiding intention to the Athletic mind to carry out the movement. When the Thinking mind tries to control movement directly, all it does is interfere with the Athletic mind.

The Three Minds model helps explain why using mechanical swing thoughts during performance is counterproductive. Mechanical thoughts arise in the Thinking mind. When the Thinking mind attempts to force a specific movement on the Athletic mind, it creates conflicting objectives, a split in focus, and confusion. You don't need to consciously direct your legs in order to walk. The idea of moving to a different location is enough.

Developing awareness of how each of your three minds contributes to performance will give you a level of control in pressure situations you may not suspect existed, because you'll know which area of specialty should be doing what, and when.

The Thinking Mind

The **Thinking Mind** specializes in conscious thought and intellectual reasoning, and is referred to as our executive function. Located in the neocortex and prefrontal cortex, it is the newest part of our brain from an evolutionary standpoint.

The Thinking mind has a rational side that is brilliant with facts, figures, data, and logic. It is great at diagnosis, solving complex problems and breaking down technique into minute parts. It also has a creative side that loves imagery, artistry, intuition, and focusing attention.

It is the source of language, as well as concepts and ideas. It is capable of working in the future (creating a strategy and imagining the shot), in the present (being task focused), and in the past (post-shot analysis of results).

Its involvement is also critical in the first stage of learning a new technique, which includes understanding detailed concepts such as swing plane, grip, stance, setup, alignment, posture, and ball position. It links conscious thought with short-term memory, which is critical in initial learning. It functions best when the body is in a static state – in other words, when we aren't attempting an athletic movement such as swinging a golf club.

Thinking mind strengths to use with golf:

- Analysis: Evaluating lie, yardage, conditions, and situations
- Calculation: Factoring variables to determine yardages, pick targets, club selection and shot type
- Prediction: Deciding intention, where the ball should end up, and how best to get it there
- Creation: Imagining shot, shape, trajectory
- Synthesis: Creating final strategy by integrating analysis, calculations and intent
- Language: Using positive talk to reinforce intent, commitment and confidence
- Focus: Concentrating awareness to the present moment and just the shot at hand

At the same time, the Thinking mind has a number of weaknesses. An anonymous athlete once said, "*Give yourself enough time to think and you can talk yourself out of just about anything.*" Analysis can lead to paralysis. Indecision can lead to overcontrol. Technical swing information can overpower creative imagery as well as sensory feedback. Judgment can cause negative emotional reactions. Too much internal dialog creates confusion. Too much negative dialog distracts from focus and confidence.

Thinking mind weaknesses to avoid with golf:

- Physical execution: Minimize or eliminate thoughts that interfere with, or attempt to control, physical movements

- Emotional interference: As a rule, avoid negative thoughts and interpretations. Instead, channel thoughts in a positive direction with positive outcomes

Once you select a strategy that fits the situation and your game, the Thinking mind steps aside, allowing the Athletic mind to execute the shot. The Thinking mind is very busy before the swing, disengaged during the swing, and busy again during the post-shot routine.

The Emotional Mind

The **Emotional Mind** is centered in the limbic system, and more specifically the amygdala. Its purpose is to ensure our well-being. It does that by focusing our attention to an event, and then motivating us to respond. Using neurotransmitters to activate our sympathetic nervous system, it triggers physiological changes in muscle tone and energy levels through the release of hormones and neurochemicals. The resulting experience can be either positive, as with joy or satisfaction, or negative, as with disappointment or anger.

Emotions function as a guide to help us survive and thrive. Positive emotions motivate us to continue and to do more, while negative emotions discourage us and send a message that change is needed. The more urgent the need, the more intense the reaction.

The Emotional mind is not directly linked to the sensory system nor to motor movement control. It doesn't collect information directly; rather, it reacts to information it is given. That's one reason the saying "*fake it until you make it*" actually works: keep telling yourself you are confident, and eventually the Emotional mind will believe it.

The Emotional mind is very strong and can act very quickly. When fully activated, it can flood short-term working memory and overwhelm the Thinking and the Athletic minds.

Positive emotions keep all three minds in balance and focused in the present moment. Negative emotions such as anger and frustration, on the other hand, attempt to divert focus to the past, while emotions such as anxiety and fear try to pull focus into the future.

Emotional mind strengths to use for golf:

- Positive emotions such as confidence, joy and excitement keep us present-centered.

- Positive emotions keep the Emotional mind in balance and in sync with the other two minds
- Strong, powerful and quick to react
- Can be managed, to a degree, by the information it is given

Emotional Mind limitations to avoid for golf:

- When fully activated, the Emotional mind can flood short term working memory, completely overwhelming both the Thinking and the Athletic minds
- Negative emotions pull focus out of the present moment. Negative emotions like anger and frustration are reactions to events in the past, while emotions such as anxiety and fear are reactions to events in the future
- It is not always possible to control the immediate, instinctive negative reaction to a mishit shot
- What can be controlled is the direction, intensity, and duration of the emotion
- The Emotional mind is reactive
- It is not directly linked to the sensory system or motor movement control

Any emotions that pull us out of the present moment are a source of interference. They divert focus, muddy intention, and obstruct execution. They pull our three minds out of sync.

It is certainly okay to experience every emotion – painful as some can be – as long as those emotions don't interfere with the next shot. By recognizing a negative emotion when it arrives and developing the self-awareness to be able to name it – *I'm frustrated* – you can control its ability to influence the next shot.

What you tell your Emotional mind is an important aspect of managing emotions. By gaining knowledge of your internal dialog and staying in the present, you can monitor your emotions, learn techniques for identifying harmful ones, and then cut them off or contain them before they negatively affect your performance.

It is equally important not to judge shots as good or bad. The Emotional mind interprets good or bad value judgments as helpful or harmful, and reacts accordingly. It is only through judgment that emotions become positive or negative. Train your Thinking mind to interpret results as factual data to mitigate the impact of value judgments being passed to the Emotional mind.

You can also proactively develop positive emotional reactions and habits. Taylor Clark said in his book *Nerve*:

> *"The switch to a friendlier view of fear is more than mere sleight of hand. Studies of everyone from classical musicians to competitive swimmers found no difference at all between elites and novices in the intensity of their pre-performance anxiety; the poised, top-flight performers, however, were far more likely to describe their fear as an aid to success. No matter what skill we're trying to improve under pressure – working on deadline, public speaking, staying cool on a first date – learning to work with fear instead of against it is a transformative shift."*

Your Emotional mind may go in and out of sync with your Thinking and Athletic minds during the round. Your Emotional mind needs only to be in sync for the time it takes to prepare for and hit the shot. You are in control of whether your emotions use you or you use your emotions, underscoring the importance of monitoring and regulating your internal dialog.

The Athletic Mind

The Athletic mind's most important function is to execute the movement. The Athletic mind resides in long-term motor memory in the motor cortex (learned technical skills) and cerebellum. It regulates balance, tempo, coordination and automatic play. The Athletic mind is directly connected to skilled voluntary movement. If movement is going to happen, the Athletic mind will be the one to do it.

Our Athletic mind bathes in sensory feedback. It receives input directly from our kinesthetic, visual, auditory, and tactile senses. By some estimates, our senses process 10 million bits per second, including feedback from eyes, skin, ears, smell, and taste. We connect with the environment through our senses, not through our conscious minds. The Athletic mind senses, the Thinking mind analyzes, the Emotional mind cares.

Full sensory information – sight, feel, sound and touch – is required to reach top performance. During play we are intensely engaged in the process, constantly sifting and evaluating information like lie, stance, wind, moisture, distance, trajectory, target, and ball flight.

When it's time to swing, though, great players forget about data and rely on what their Athletic mind tells them is the right shot for the conditions. Playing golf in the Athletic mind requires more than the absence of technical thoughts. It requires

- The collaboration of your senses so that you are visually aware of the target, the ball flight, and your own swing
- Kinesthetic awareness of your body position, balance, swing plane, and tempo
- Anticipatory auditory awareness of the sound of a well-struck shot or the ball falling into the cup
- Tactile awareness of the feel of the club as it strikes through the ball and pulls you into a well-balanced finishing position

It is okay to acknowledge all the potential negative outcomes conceived by the Thinking mind. It is okay for the Emotional mind to be anxious. But when the Athletic mind gets too much information from the Thinking mind, and too much negative feedback from the Emotional mind, it becomes bewildered. Too much input, with too many conflicting action priorities, creates paralysis.

When it is time to execute, the Athletic mind performs best when it has clarity about a single objective from the Thinking mind and positive feelings about the strategy from the Emotional mind.

Creating a communication channel between the Thinking mind and the Athletic mind is one of the goals of execution drills. Imagery is one of the most commonly used techniques to facilitate this communication. Simple, clear, congruent input from the Thinking and Emotional minds allows the Athletic mind to operate to the height of its ability.

In an ideal world, the three minds might work together like this:

Stage 1: The Thinking Mind determines strategy by

- *Engages the rational left brain for analytics: evaluates the lie, yardage and situation, factoring in variables like wind, moisture, elevation, pin placement, or target*
- *Determines the risk/reward options by balancing the needs of the shot vs. one's skills and abilities*

- *Comes up with a solution/strategy*
- *Uses the creative right brain to visualize the shot or imagine what the outcome should look like*

Stage 2: Emotional Mind approves

- *Somewhere in this process the Emotional Mind provides a stamp of approval. Or not. Usually as a result of evaluating the risk/reward and consequences*

Stage 3: The Athletic Mind Executes

- *Receives image of the shot from the Thinking Mind*
- *Begins to a feel for the movement that will produce the desired outcome*
- *Physically rehearses the movement that matches the image, synchronizing the image with the feel of the swing, and completing the handoff from the Thinking mind*
- *Initiates the set-up routine steps and gets athletically ready to hit the shot*
- *Carries out the movement by executing the swing, which it is pretty good at doing all by itself. Any participation at this point by the other two minds usually causes confusion and destroys consistency. Unfortunately the Thinking mind loves to give last-minute instructions, while the Emotional mind is always ready to throw in a "gotcha" during the swing*

Stage 4: All minds collaborate to analyze results

- *After the shot, all three minds work together to process the results*
- *The Athletic mind provides physical and sensory feedback*
- *Thinking mind analyzes results and feedback*
- *Emotional mind reacts*
- *Thinking mind completes the post-shot analysis, issues instructions to adjust or reinforce based on its analysis, and prepares for the next shot*

If you want to have a little fun with it, you could think of the three minds as the Nerd, the Basket Case, and the Jock. The Nerd takes care of strategy, the Basket Case is responsible for intensity, and the Jock is in charge of action. Individually maybe not so great. But together, they make a formidable team.

The key takeaway from the Three Minds model is to allow each mind to be in charge of the tasks for which they specialize, and keep them from interfering with the other minds when it is their turn.

Playing clutch golf requires the collaboration of all three Minds working together in harmony. The Three Minds model provides insight into the strengths of each mind and how they facilitate performance. Equally as important, the model provides insight about when each mind should *not* be involved.

Awareness Exercise: Opposite-Hand Signature

Try this exercise of writing your signature with each hand to experience the stages of motor learning, as well as observe your three minds in action.

First sign your name on a piece of paper as you normally would. Note how little "thinking" goes into the movement. You just put your pen to paper and sign. That's the type of automatic execution we'd like to see for our golf swings.

Now try signing your name with your off hand.

Suddenly an otherwise "automatic" process becomes significantly more challenging.

Since it is an unfamiliar motor movement, you have to consciously think through every aspect of the process. Just figuring out how to hold the pen may take a while and involve considerable thought as well as trial and error. Then you have to determine what angle the pen needs to meet the paper. Then you have to figure out how to move the pen across the paper. That's your Thinking mind at work, and you'll notice a lot of back and forth communication between your Thinking and Athletic minds.

Trying to recreate all the unique loops and swirls of your normal signature will seem like an impossible task at first. You may even become frustrated. More than likely your off-hand signature will not look anything like your original. It certainly won't be as smooth and flowing. This is the Cognitive stage of motor learning, characterized by heavy thinking, much trial and error, and considerable inaccuracy.

If you keep at it, however, some parts of the process will come together. As you solve more execution issues, your Thinking mind will pass more and more of the execution to the Athletic mind. You'll move into Stage 2 of motor learning, the Associative stage, as various actions are integrated into the larger movement pattern.

Switch back to your normal hand and note again how effortlessly you sign. There is no intervention by the Thinking mind. The intent is enough. This level of automaticity is Stage 3 of motor learning. The action is automatic, fluid, accurate, and consistent.

This is a fun opportunity to not only observe the motor learning process, but also to develop an awareness of your three minds working together (and sometimes at odds!).

It's also an example of why automatic execution is the ultimate goal for your golf swing.

****

Motor Learning models help us understand where we are in the skill acquisition continuum. They highlight our physical and mental progress and the associated activities. But what is missing for clutch play is emotional influence, especially when it creates pressure.

Understanding the gamut of the emotional landscape allows you to pinpoint your ideal emotional playing state, and that awareness is an important tool in your emotional management skill set. Not all emotions create negative interference. In fact, we often use positive descriptions for emotions that help us play well. Everybody's best performances happen at a unique emotional intensity level, ranging from calm and even-keeled to pumped up and excited.

The next model focuses specifically on emotions. The emotional landscape provides a framework for understanding the broad scope of all emotions, and a process to identify your ideal emotional intensity level.

Your Ideal Emotional Intensity Level

Think back to a time when you played really well. What were your emotions like? How would you describe them? Were you serene, excited, or more even-keeled?

By naming your emotional state during your best performances, you can identify your ideal emotional intensity level. Assigning a number between 1 and 10 for low to high allows you to envision a range of intensity where you play best.

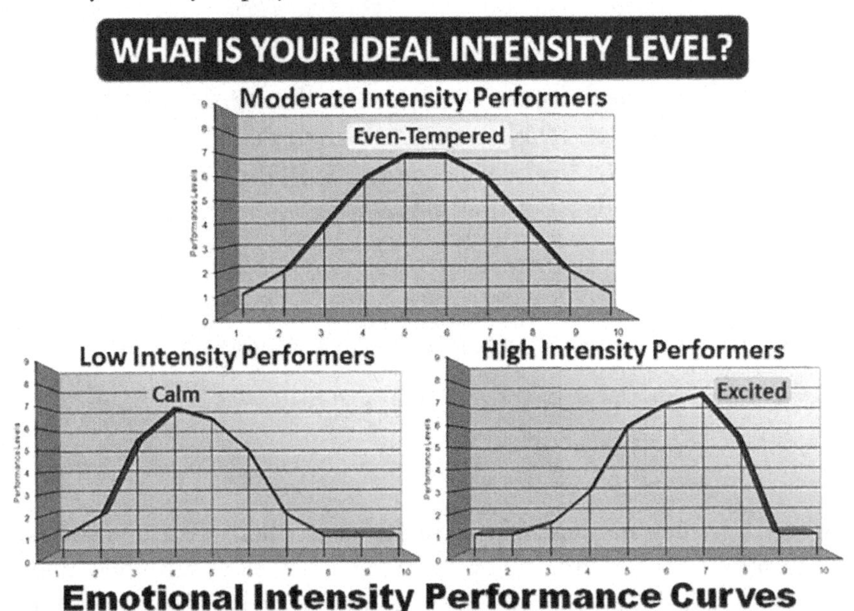

Emotional Intensity Performance Curves

Some players perform best when they are as mellow as Dustin Johnson and Ernie Els. Some play better when they are excited and fist-pumping like Tiger. Some play best when they are even-keeled: not too high and not too low. The more often you play from your ideal emotional level, the more reliably you'll execute at a higher level.

Players who describe themselves as calm perform best with minimal emotional activation. High-intensity players, who describe themselves as fired up, need the boost they get from high emotions. Your goal is to identify the level you play best, and then construct routines and habits that consistently drive you toward your ideal emotional state:

- Calm players are likely to use techniques like relaxation breathing and imagery
- High intensity players are likely to use highly motivating positive self-talk
- Even-keeled players may find centering their mind and body in the present moment to be the best approach

Managing your emotions is the art of consistently executing from your ideal emotional intensity level. Choose a word like calm, cool, focused, excited, keen, or another that describes your optimal emotional performance state. With that emotional state in mind, dedicate part of your practice time to emotional management. Use your pre-shot, post-shot, and in-between routines to discover a process that enables you to manage yourself back to that level, particularly when adversity strikes.

Managing emotions is one of the trickiest skills to master. We don't get to practice managing emotions until they are happening, and it is very challenging to maintain objective awareness in the heat of the battle. Emotions can flood the Thinking and Athletic minds so thoroughly that bringing the appropriate mental tools into play can seem impossible.

Take heart in knowing that every athlete experiences anxiety and fear, disappointment and resignation. Just knowing you have an ideal emotional playing state, though, provides assurance that there is a path to get you to your happy place no matter the current situation.

Develop a positive attitude toward anxiety, fear, and nervousness. It's not as though the emotions go away, even for clutch players. It's just that clutch players have figured out how to use them to their advantage, compartmentalize them, reframe them, ignore them, or go ahead and hit the shot anyway. One way or another, they find a way to do what they need to do.

Paying attention to emotional reactions develops the self-awareness necessary to learn what works and what doesn't. It also allows players to refine "what works best" to keep getting better at it. The process of building emotional management skills deepens confidence.

Confidence Models

It seems a truism that you perform better when you play with confidence. The dictionary defines it as "*a feeling of self-assurance and belief in one's abilities.*" For some players, the search for confidence is the holy grail.

To describe confidence we use words such as trust, belief, positivity, certainty, heart, fearlessness, nerve, poise, reliance, resilience, and faith. The words describe feelings, which indicate confidence is rooted in the Emotional mind. Since your Emotional mind does not interface directly with the outside world, it can only react to internal input from your conscious mind and physical senses.

Therefore what your Thinking mind sends to your Emotional mind is critical.

Ninety-five percent of your emotions – the way you feel about yourself from moment to moment – are determined by the way you talk to yourself. We average about 1,700 words of dialogue running through our mind every minute. Your job is to make sure the internal dialog directed to your Emotional mind is positive and optimistic.

When you prepare correctly, you have a wealth of positive experience to draw from to create a stream of positive dialog. You can choose to focus on all the good things and positive results. Your Emotional mind, not knowing any better, will respond with positive feelings.

Developing confidence is a key step in turning into a clutch player. Confidence builds resilience, strengthens belief in yourself, motivates you to stretch your capabilities, overcomes negativity, promotes a positive mental outlook, and minimizes interference. Playing with confidence is a key ingredient of peak performances.

Then there is the matter of degree: Are you 100% confident? Or are you somewhere in between? What about on different shots? Or with different clubs?

Most of the literature talks about confidence as if it were an on/off switch. Either you are confident or you are not. Our experience, and that of client athletes, is that it there are degrees of confidence. You can be more confident or less confident depending on the circumstances. There is, however, one type of confidence that is reliable and long-lasting: internal confidence.

Confidence: Internal vs. External

Dr. Albaugh pioneered the concept of Internal vs. External confidence to give athletes a way to develop unshakable confidence and remain positive in any situation.

External confidence is the type we are most familiar with. It's based on the athlete's immediate past performance: the last shot or two you've hit. External confidence, however, is fleeting. All it takes is one bad shot and your confidence can evaporate. Yet it's the type nearly always discussed by commentators. External confidence isn't bad; it's just difficult to sustain.

The more enduring type of belief comes from internal confidence.

Internal confidence isn't about thinking you can; it's *knowing* you can. Internal confidence is developed through quality practice. You have control over your internal confidence because you have to put in the time and effort to develop it. You don't need a perfect technical swing. It has nothing to do with how superbly or how poorly you hit the previous shot. Confidence is an acquired psychological state of mind nurtured through practice.

Three C's of Confidence

Another way to understand confidence arose from (author) Eric Jones' Sport Psychology Master's thesis. Participants found a direct relationship between the quality of their shot and the level of their confidence: the more often they chose a strategy that gave them confidence, the more often they hit higher quality shots.

A key finding was the identification of three underlying factors that led to greater confidence in strategy decisions: comfort, concentration, and commitment. The three C's of confidence. Before each shot, the study participants asked themselves three simple questions:

- **Comfort**: *Am I comfortable*? If they didn't feel comfortable over a shot, they learned to ask themselves what shot they *would* feel comfortable hitting. Then they switched to the comfortable shot
- **Concentration***: Can I concentrate*? If they couldn't concentrate, they learned to identify the sources of interference. This required them to spend considerable time listening to the inner dialog running through their mind to develop awareness around their thoughts and thought patterns
- **Commitment**: *Can I commit*? If they couldn't commit, they sought clarity: did they have the right strategy? Or was there something about the club selection, shot shape, hazards, lie, conditions, or skill level required that prevented them from staying committed? They also learned a "just do it anyway" mentality

When the study participants used the Three C's to evaluate their shot choices, they realized they had much more control over their confidence. They began to make different strategy decisions when they recognized they were at a less than optimal level on one of the Three C's. If one parameter in particular described why they were not confident in a situation, identifying the underlying cause helped them choose a strategy that gave them a higher degree of confidence.

They also learned that commitment is like a trump card. When all else failed they could override comfort and concentration and make a confident swing anyway, as long as they stayed committed. The old adage of "fake it 'til you make it" worked. After all, their Emotional mind didn't know any better. It just did what it was told. By the end of the 12-week study, all five participants recorded a new career-low score.

How Do We Build Confidence?

Internal confidence begins with the unwavering belief that your mental and physical game fundamentals are correct, and that you have practiced them properly. Internal confidence built through good preparation is, as Coach Carroll noted, the first step on the path to confidence.

Confidence is strengthened by a nonjudgmental approach to your shots, by positive internal dialog, and by positive imagery. It is developed systematically through practicing properly, projecting positive imagery, clearing your mind of mechanical swing thoughts, using positive self-talk, having a positive attitude, maintaining great posture, and trust in your preparation. As Dallas Cowboys legend Roger Staubach said:

> *"Confidence doesn't come out of nowhere. It's a result of hours and days and weeks and years of constant work and dedication."*

Use this checklist to strengthen your confidence:

- Have a positive attitude
- Use Positive Self-Talk
- Learn from mistakes
- Have realistic expectations
- Visualize positive outcomes
- Act with confidence
- Believe in yourself
- Prepare systematically
- Maintain motivation

External and Internal confidence are most effective when used in concert with each other. If you get on a roll and your external confidence is soaring, ride it for all it's worth. When you miss a shot, fall back on the internal confidence you earned through practice and preparation.

Coach's Advice

1. Follow Coach Dunning's advice to find a style that works for you, then build your game around it.
2. Use motor learning models to identify your stage of learning so that you can tailor your activities to provide the right kind of feedback and set appropriate expectations.
3. Determine your emotional intensity level and choose a word that describes it. Use routines and mental techniques to manage your emotions so that you execute from that level as often as you can.
4. Build your internal confidence through quality practice. Play with more confidence by using three C's of confidence (comfort, concentration, commitment) to make better strategy and shot decisions.
5. Understand the role each of your three minds (Thinking, Emotional and Athletic) plays in both learning and performing. Keep them in balance.

Chapter 10: Developing Clutch Resilience

Mistakes are always a challenge to deal with, and coming up short in big situations tends to affect us more profoundly than missing any other shot. As we've noted, playing to your statistical average is all it takes to be clutch. But that also means you're guaranteed to fail a certain percentage of the time.

In this chapter, we'll identify skills that will help you deal with mistakes and losses. Chief among those skills is resilience – the ability to take it on the chin and come back swinging even harder.

Pete Carroll embraces excellence at the core of their team culture. But along with developing the ability to be gracious in victory comes a need for the opposite: the ability to be graceful in defeat. Resilience is the hallmark of being, as Carroll says, "*the epitome of poise.*"

Pete Carroll's Resilience Coaching

In the 49th Super Bowl, the Seahawks trailed New England 24-28 with time running out. The Seahawks had the ball on the 2-yard line, but only 26 seconds remained on the clock. With one time out left, Coach Carroll had to make a decision on second down: pass, or run?

This was a situation they had practiced before. The Seahawks make a regular habit of game-planning a variety of scenarios for every kind of situation, including potential game-winning plays with the clock running out. Like this one.

Coach Carroll was clear on the choices they had to consider and the decision they had to make.

- If they called a running play and didn't make it, they still had the time out. But they were likely to get only one more play after that.

- On the other hand, if they called a pass and it was incomplete, the clock would stop, and they'd have time to run two more plays. They'd still have one time-out.

Carroll called the pass play.

Malcolm Butler of the Patriots jumped the pass and intercepted it.

Game over.

Talking heads felt it was the wrong call. But was it?

> *"I don't ever think of it as the worst call, reflects Carroll. "I think it was one of the best plays that somebody ever made. The play didn't work out for us, but it did for them."*

You can't win them all. Which means you need two things:

1. A process to achieve clarity in your decision-making, so that you have solid reasoning behind your strategy. Carroll said, *"We were clear in that moment because we had prepared for it. We knew what we were going to do. We had the whole sequence in mind. We were calm and poised about it."*
2. The sportsmanship to handle defeat with grace. "*All you can hope for is to put yourself in the best position for the opportunity that you've prepared for. You've clearly thought your way through it, you've made a decision like you had planned on. If it doesn't work out, it didn't work out. I think you can walk away from the situation and you move on. You can regain your stride and you can get back to clear thinking and your next opportunity.*"

You're going to fail in big situations. There's a good chance you'll blame your swing. Please don't.

Your swing doesn't change much from shot to shot. Not on its own. Your *thinking* may change, and that may *cause* something in the swing to change. But habits resist change. The collection of habitual movement patterns you've established that make your swing what it is today, remain consistent when there is no interference.

The most obvious reason for breakdowns under pressure isn't your swing technique; it's your inner game. Jaime Diaz in *Golf Digest* writes:

> *"Pressure takes a greater toll in sports that require fine motor skills. Choking is more prevalent among pitchers and hitters in baseball, shooters in basketball choke, and tennis players. And because no sport*

> *has a smaller margin for physical error than golf – be it hitting a fairway target 300 yards away or coaxing in a slick left-to-right eight footer – golfers have a harder fight against choking than other athletes. Because golfers are more alone and exposed and have more time to think than other athletes, pressure is a bigger enemy and choking is a given."*

But is pressure necessarily bad?

Clutch Resilience

Resilience is an integral part of being clutch. It's your ability to bounce back, recover quickly, be adaptable, stay flexible, and roll with the punches. It comes from the Latin *resilio*, meaning "to spring back," and is "*the positive ability to adapt to the consequences of failure*" (Wikipedia). Resilience is a choice, which tells us your ability to bounce back is totally within your control.

Be realistic about your capabilities. It is impossible to be successful in *every* clutch situation. If you made 66% of your putts from six feet you'd be at the PGA Tour average. But you'd still fail one-third of the time. A baseball player with a batting average of .333 would be a superstar, even though he fails two-thirds of the time.

How you fail is not important. Failure is unavoidable. What is important is how you bounce back. You'll have much more success bouncing back when you have a process in place before it happens.

The US Army considers resilience so important it developed a Master Resilience Training course for its 1.1 million soldiers. The goal of the training is:

> *"To teach them they can be in control of their actions and thoughts during events that are extremely difficult to handle," according to Sgt. 1st Class Manuel Torres-Cortes. "The benefit of the training is that Soldiers will build an internal strength, enabling them to focus and react to situations more clearly with positive results."*

Clutch players use purposeful training to develop the internal strength that fuels resilience. Consciously choosing to maintain a positive attitude is how you stay resilient and recover with poise.

What Do You Think?

For some golfers pressure is bad. For others, not so much.

It depends on what you think.

Each golfer must determine how pressure will affect his/her game. If you desire to be a clutch player, we encourage you to embrace the potential power inherent in clutch situations and use it to your advantage.

One of the keys to being clutch is your attitude, and particularly your attitude toward pressure. Does the pressure of a challenging situation step up your play, or does it cause you to collapse? Your attitude toward pressure is an important part of the answer.

Note that it is not until we begin to talk about clutch *players* that the term pressure becomes part of the definition. Situations and shots have consequences, but it is the player who interprets it as having pressure. Cognitive scientist Sian Beilock wrote in *Choke*:

> *"It is not the pressure in a pressure situation that distracts us into performing poorly," Beilock said. "The pressure makes us worry and want to control our actions too much. And you cannot think your way through a routine, practiced action, like making a three-foot putt."*

The players who come up big in pivotal moments learn to use pressure in a positive way, as Taylor Clark wrote in his book *Nerve:*

> *"The thing that separates cool-headed and poised people from the rest of us isn't the quantity of anxiety they feel, but their relationship with their fears. Either through instinct or hard-won wisdom, these people realize that fear isn't trying to hurt them – it's trying to help them stay safe, succeed, and thrive. Fear, they see, is not our enemy."*

The Pressure Performer Bell Curve

Research shows that for any group of players there is a bell curve distribution of performance levels under pressure. Some players will respond poorly and underperform. Some will use the situation to thrive and find new and higher levels of play. Everybody else will perform somewhere in between.

Some players on the pressure performance bell curve, about 15%-20%, experience a catastrophic drop in performance. In other words, they choke. Disastrously.

About the same number of players, 15%-20%, actually thrive under pressure. They love crucial moments, and their positive attitude toward pressure builds resilience.

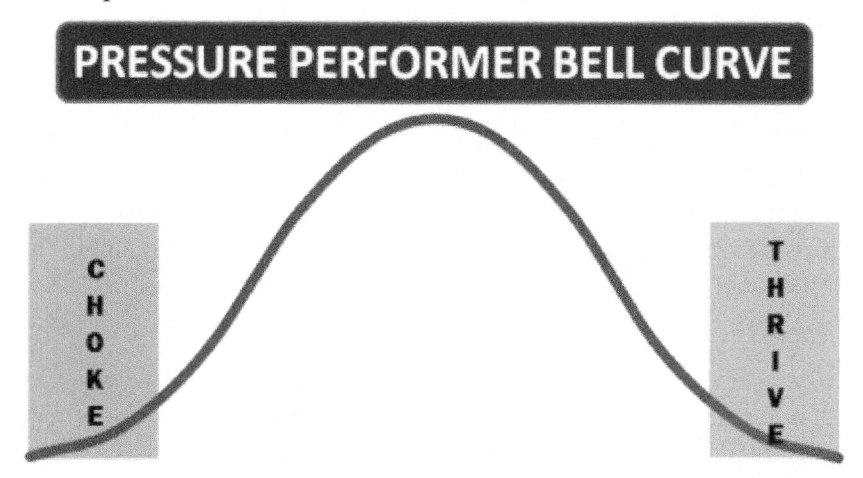

In between there is a reason the rest of performances fit closer to the average on the bell curve. Wherever you fall on the curve, thought, remember that you are not stuck there. You *can* move your performance to the high end. As psychologist Tim Woodman said in his book *Extreme Fear:*

> *"When people are low in cognitive anxiety or worry, the difference between their best performance and their worst performance is not very big. They can perform pretty well, but it's not fantastic, and it's not crap. But if you put them in a very high-worry situation, like the Olympic Games, what you find is that their best performance is significantly better than before and their worst performance is significantly worse."*

If you interpret pressure as a bad thing, it will be.

If you interpret pressure as a good thing, it will be.

Your interpretation of the situation is one of the few things over which you have complete control. Choosing to embrace pressure as a good thing will help move you to the thrive end of the bell curve.

As John Doyle said in *Baseball Training Secrets:*

> *"If you think of pressure as bad, your body will become tight, your heart rate will increase significantly and a great deal of the hormone cortisol will be released. A chance of you coming through in the clutch is slim to none."*

It's easy to forget that every athlete experiences fear. We tend to think we are all alone with our anxiety. Legendary basketball center Bill Russell reportedly threw up before every game. *Every game.* Eagles quarterback Donovan McNabb and Bills quarterback Jim Kelly were similarly affected. Martina Navratilova had butterflies before every match, even after being ranked the No. 1 tennis player in the world for over six years.

Rather than think of pressure as bad, we want you to use it to your advantage. It is the response to pressure that affects our play. Pressure can improve your level of play, and all it may require is that you change the way you think about it. As Hamlet said:

"There is nothing either good or bad, but thinking makes it so."

As you evaluate your attitude toward pressure, fear and anxiety, keep in mind that it is not about being undefeated; it's about being undaunted. Navy seal Brandon Webb said:

> *"Going through SEAL training taught me that it's okay to fall down three times, as long as you get up four. This is a good philosophy for most things in life."*

Pressure can knock you down, but it won't knock you out, as long as you keep getting back up. Martina Navratilova's *Sports Illustrated* article, *Learn To Love The Battle*, describes how she came to recognize the butterflies as a sign that she was excited about the match. She began to look forward to the butterflies because it meant she was ready to play at a high level.

Every athlete experiences anxiety and fear. Strong emotions don't go away, even for clutch players. Clutch players have just figured how to manage emotions by compartmentalizing them, reframing them, ignoring them, or simply deciding to do it anyway.

How do you become more resilient? Is it even possible to get the butterflies to fly in formation?

Dealing With Mistakes

The first step in bouncing back is acknowledging that you are going to make mistakes. You are not going to hit every shot, make every putt, or win every match. The way you deal with your mistakes plays an important role in your growth as a clutch player. As Juli Inkster said, the way we recover from mistakes is what makes us champions.

Carol Dweck's landmark book *Mindset* provides guidance through her explanation of fixed vs. growth mindsets:

- Fixed mindset individuals believe their abilities are set. They treat setbacks as catastrophic, take failures personally, get frustrated easily, feel they'll never get any better, and give up sooner. They associate failure with outcomes and avoid situations that might expose perceived shortcomings.
- Growth mindset individuals, on the other hand, believe their abilities and skills can be developed through effort and persistence. They view setbacks as challenges and opportunities to learn. Failures merely point out areas to improve, try again, or explore different approaches. Growth mindset individuals stay motivated longer, maintain better focus, show greater creativity, and have less stress. Coaches also play a significant role in fostering a growth mindset by reinforcing attitude, motivation and commitment to the process.

Nothing dulls the sting of a loss, though. The question is this: How will you respond?

> *"Failure can be a painful experience. But it doesn't define you. It's a problem to be faced, dealt with, and learned from,"* noted Dweck.

Adopt a growth mindset that views mistakes as temporary, specific to that one shot, and not necessarily representative of the way you typically perform. Treat success, on the other hand, as a better indicator of your usual play.

Pete Carroll's Seahawks could have viewed their loss in Super Bowl 49 as a crushing failure. Instead, they chose to treat it as an opportunity to display a different kind of skill:

> *"The epitome of poise: an opportunity to demonstrate how to deal with extraordinary disappointment and try to do it really well."*

Carroll's decision to take responsibility for his decision, live with the consequences, and demonstrate grace in defeat, showed the mark of a true champion. It's also an example of why so many clutch golf skills are equally valuable life skills.

The crux of dealing effectively with mistakes is to develop a process to manage your emotions and thoughts. Prepare it in advance. Know what you are going to do and how you are going to do it. It's too risky to believe you'll make the best decisions in highly intense and emotional situations. The time to decide how to handle emotions is before they happen.

It's going to take a significant amount of experimentation to find out what works best for you. Likely you'll wind up with multiple ways to deal with setbacks. There are as many emotions as there are clutch situations. When you make a mistake, ask yourself if you did everything you could to the best of your abilities. Then ask yourself what you can learn so that next time your best can be even better. Find the positives. Be a life-long learner.

You may lose the match, but you will never lose the lesson.

Post-Shot Routines

One of your most important resilience tools will be a post-shot routine. Those few seconds after a shot are your best opportunity to analyze the results, learn from them, and manage post-shot reactions. Having a consciously designed post-shot routine gives you the option of using a variety of mental skills, enabling you to recover quickly from mistakes.

Execute your post-shot routine right away, before the memory of the swing fades. You only have a few seconds to recreate the feel of the shot, so that you can compare what you intended to what really happened. If there was a difference, you want to know why, so you can make corrections.

With a little practice, you can run through your post-shot routine very quickly to get the feedback you need. You'll learn more from each shot, have an easier time identifying issues and cataloging tendencies that can be added to practice sessions. Knowing that you'll address issues later will help you let go of mistakes faster when you play.

But don't forget to appreciate good shots! Use your post-shot routine to take a moment and absorb the sound of a well-struck shot, the feel of solid impact, and the sight of the ball bouncing down the fairway or curving toward the target and coming to rest near the pin. These moments allow you to capture the full sensory feedback and feel of good shots, which helps embed them in long-term memory, where they are available for instant recall whenever you need them. Having a memory bank full of successful shots will help you keep your current shot in perspective.

In-Between Routines

The vast majority of your time on the golf course will be in-between time. This seldom-discussed time can be tremendously productive for clutch players when used purposefully. It can be equally destructive if channeled the wrong direction.

Just as you have a routine before the shot and a routine after the shot, develop a routine for in-between time. Your in-between routine's purpose is to bridge the gap from your post shot routine to your next shot. It is a time to:

- Let go of the previous shot
- Work yourself back into your happy place and your ideal emotional intensity level
- Begin to prepare for the next shot

While it is helpful to analyze shots to gain insights, it is counterproductive to dwell excessively on past shots. Limit the time spent on post-shot analysis. When the analysis spins off into "*coulda, woulda, shoulda,*" it leads to doubts and recriminations, which affect future play.

Instead, suspend judgment and treat the results as facts and data. Turn the results into objective feedback by assigning numerical values instead of judgments. Rather than say it was a good shot, say it was a 7 on a scale of 10. Rather than say it was a bad shot, call it a 4 out of 10.

Subjective scales are internal measures and are only meaningful to the player. But they are a way to quantify otherwise non-measurable thoughts, feelings, and actions. Once you can measure something, you can manage it. And if you can manage it, you can improve it.

Your in-between time is also an opportunity to manage your emotional landscape. Since you know your ideal emotional intensity number, you can "take your temperature" en route to the next shot. When used consistently, your in-between routine will provide invaluable insight into your tendencies and trends. Whenever you stray too far from your ideal emotional playing level, use the in-between time to draw on your mental skills toolkit to get yourself back to your happy place, where you know you perform best.

Use your in-between time to return to a present-time state. Resilience is bouncing back, and the state to bounce back to is being present-centered.

The first step is getting centered in the present moment. Your body can only act in the "now," so getting your mind centered in the "now" will help get you in sync. With mind and body centered in the moment, it is possible to bring your full focus to the next shot. For your mind and body there is only one time that matters: now. The important skill is getting your attention back to the task at hand.

Dealing With Nerves

When you get nervous, your body reacts in a predictable fashion:

- Your heart rate increases
- Your breathing becomes rapid and shallow. Shallow breathing means air enters only the upper part of the chest, which doesn't deliver enough oxygen deep into the lungs
- Consequently you feel short of breath, even while breathing rapidly. The body interprets high, upper-chest breathing as "panic" breathing
- Your sympathetic nervous system is activated, releasing hormones like adrenaline and cortisol, preparing you for a "fight or flight" response
- Blood is re-routed to the large muscle groups and away from the stomach and skin. With less blood in the skin and stomach you get cold, clammy sweat and butterflies
- Blood pressure goes up and sugar is released to the muscles for added strength or rapid response
- Your senses become heightened, your pupils dilate, hearing becomes more acute, and touch is more sensitive. You are processing more data, leading to a feeling of distraction
- Your field of attention becomes so broad, it gets scattered. You attempt to focus intently on too many environmental and physical cues in too many different directions
- Paradoxically, with less oxygen your brain becomes less efficient at processing information and quickly becomes overloaded. You

begin to worry about performance and obsess over non-essential details. You may even worry about worrying

- You become tense and you lose fluidity and automaticity as you try to bear down and consciously control each movement

And yet even with all these symptoms, we somehow manage to swing the club and get a shot off. Learning to recognize the signs of nervousness is a vital part of your self-awareness skill set.

The Big Three Mental Skills

There are many sport psychology techniques available to help you deal with any number of mental and emotional challenges and the responses they elicit. Explore techniques and tools freely. When you find techniques that improve the pillars of focus, intention, or trust, add them to your toolkit.

Three mental techniques in particular tend to be used most often during play: relaxation breathing, visualization, and positive self-talk. The three big techniques help control thoughts, manage emotions, and center the body. They can be used to supercharge performance skills, enhancing your ability to execute with higher focus, intention and trust.

Every player we know uses at least one of these techniques. Most use all three, plus whatever else they've discovered that helps them. If you are not purposefully using the big three techniques, they should be the first mental skills to add to your toolkit.

Relaxation Breathing

Relaxation breathing, as the name implies, is a breath taken with the intention of calming and relaxing. It can also be used to focus.

A relaxation breath, done properly, is a deep breath that activates the diaphragm, expanding your abdomen and drawing air deep into the lungs. More oxygen enters the bloodstream and gets carried to the brain, helping the mind operate more effectively.

Whether you call it a yoga breath, circle breath, or diaphragmatic breathing, activating the diaphragm tells the body to release DHEA, acetylcholine and cholinesterase, which counteract the effects of adrenaline and cortisol. These hormones are the antidote to stress.

Relaxation breathing is also used while performing body scans to identify areas of excess muscular tension. Focus on tense areas, and then consciously relax those muscles during the exhale.

Relaxation breathing helps sharpen your focus. Paying attention to the sound of your breath, heartbeat or tense muscle group narrows your focus, allowing thoughts and emotions to fade into the background. Your senses are already heightened when you are under stress. That extra awareness can be used to intensify your focus.

Breathing helps center you in the present – both physically and mentally. It is impossible to worry about the future when you concentrate on the act of breathing.

Use relaxation breathing at any time throughout your round. Use it to:

- Get present-centered while walking to your next shot
- Start your pre-shot routine
- Narrow your focus to the target and shot
- Relax your body prior to stepping into the shot
- Re-focus if you get distracted prior to swinging
- Let go of unwanted tension
- Process and analyze results after the shot
- Counteract emotions during your post-shot routine
- Get yourself to your happy place during in-between time

Coach's Note: A breath taken high into your upper chest only, without activating the diaphragm, will be interpreted by the autonomous system as a panic breath. Even though you think you may be drawing in lots of air, the oxygen is not delivered deep into your lungs. Panic breathing will actually put *more* adrenaline and cortisol into your bloodstream, causing an even greater physical reaction. It will have the opposite effect of calming. Perform your relaxation breathing correctly by expanding your diaphragm and drawing air deep into your lungs.

Visualization

Visualization is the act of imagining or recreating a moment, event or idea in your mind. It's your ability to pre-create a shot in your mind's eye before it happens. Dr. Richard Keefe wrote in his book *On The Sweet Spot*:

> *"The idea that an internal image of action can improve the ease and accuracy of that action is now well accepted in sport science and neuroscience. It helps athletes "stop monitoring their movements and just let them happen on their own."*

Jack Nicklaus's oft-cited quote is one of the best descriptions of a master visualizer and well worth applying to your pre-shot routine. It fits lock, load, and fire neatly.

> *"I never hit a shot, not even in practice, without having a very sharp, in-focus picture of it in my head. It's like a color movie. First, I 'see' the ball where I want it to finish, nice and white and sitting up high on bright green grass. Then the scene quickly changes and I 'see' the ball going there; its path, trajectory and shape, even its behavior on landing. Then there is a sort of a fade-out, and the next scene shows me making the kind of swing that will turn the images into reality."*

Visualizing your shot is the combined effort of the rational (left-side) and creative (right-side) parts of your brain. The left brain devises the strategy and the right brain creates the imagery – whether snapshot or movie – of how it will be done. Imagery helps to:

- Sharpen focus by giving you something specific to zero in on
- Cement intention by providing clarity about the objective
- Regulate breathing
- Slow heart rate
- Relax muscle groups
- Evoke confidence
- Foster a positive mindset
- Enhance commitment
- Limit over-thinking by directing the Thinking mind's attention to a specific task
- Manage distractions by providing a clear model for action
- Override negative thinking and emotional interference

One of the most important outcomes of visualization is to communicate your intention to the Athletic mind.

The Athletic mind does not have language capability per se, so it cannot understand words. But it *is* adept at pattern recognition. Pictures are nothing but patterns, and they are the preferred language of the Athletic mind. The clearer the picture, the more effectively the Athletic mind will understand and carry out the task.

Imagery Anchors: One of the best ways to remember images is by using imagery anchors. On the sea, anchors keep ships in place. In sports, we use anchors to keep images in place.

The best anchors use all your senses. They include sight, sound, smell, feel, and emotions. The more vivid you can make your images, the more securely anchored they will be in long term memory, where they will be easier to recall when needed.

Create as many images as you can. When you hit a shot particularly well, take a moment to anchor it in. Retain the video of the ball flying, landing and rolling to a stop. Recall the sound and feel of solid impact. Recall how relaxed you were, how sharp your concentration was, how confident you feel, how motivated you are, or how determined you felt.

The way you think and feel is directly related to performance. Create an anchor around your best performances so you can recall every aspect when you need it.

Positive Self-Talk

We have an astonishing volume of dialog running through our minds. To put it in context, we speak about 170 words per minute, and listen at 650 words per minute. But we think an order of magnitude faster at around 1,700 words per minute.

Since it only takes 1.5 seconds to make a golf swing, the obvious implication is that we are capable of 40 different thoughts during the swing. Some students report that there are times when it feels like a lot more than that.

The words you use when you talk to yourself play a major role in your emotions. As much as 95% of your emotional state at any given point in time is determined by your internal dialog. Small wonder, then, why high-performing athletes develop a variety of positive action phrases to manage their emotional outlook.

Positive self-talk generally falls into one of two categories: supportive language and task-specific instructions.

1. Supportive language includes thoughts such as *I can do this, This is my favorite shot,* or *You got this.* They are positive, encouraging and motivating.

2. Task specific talk such as *release to the target* or *smooth tempo* is an excellent way for the Thinking and Athletic minds to get in sync.

Use positive talk on yourself the same way you would with your best friend: be positive, encouraging and supportive. Use it in self-coaching to focus your attention on progress being made or ways to improve.

Centering

Centering is a concept borrowed from martial arts. It is about balance and power, both of the mind and the body. Whenever centering is mentioned throughout the book, we refer to being both mentally and physically centered.

It is critically important, though, that past and future are mental constructs. Your body only knows one time: *now*. Movement only happens in the present. If your thoughts and emotions are not in the present moment as well – if they are in the past or in the future – your mind will be out of sync with your body.

Being totally centered in the present moment is one of the keys to pulling off clutch shots.

- **Physically Centered**: Getting physically centering elicits a sense of being grounded and completely supported by the earth. It is a relaxed yet poised position of potential, where you are athletically balanced and capable of moving effortlessly in any direction. The body's center is a point between your belly button and spine. It is the source of all strength, and all movement revolves around it. Maximum power is transferred by hitting from the center. Be prepared to move immediately from athletic centering into the swing. You will be well-focused and balanced.
- **Mentally Centered**: The mind's center is in the present moment, not the past or future. In the present moment your thoughts are focused, you think clearly, and you are calm yet capable. You are fully engaged with the task at hand and there are no thoughts of what happened or what may come. Being mentally present centered has been described by Richard Baker-Roshi, a leading teacher of Zen Buddhism, as:

  "*The highest order of consciousness, the most challenging to reach, to return to, and to maintain.*"

Like any other skills, centering can be learned and refined through mindfulness practice. Mindfulness is the Zen term for having the self-awareness to stay in the present, monitor your emotions, and then apply techniques to deflect interfering thoughts and emotions before they affect performance.

Practice mindfulness whenever you practice mental centering to keep your mind and body in balance, relaxed, focused, and ready. Pausing occasionally to "stop and smell the roses" will anchor you in the present and allow you to appreciate the experience.

Keep Stats

We wish more players would keep stats on their game. Even simple stats like how many fairways and greens you hit and how many putts per round would be an immensely more helpful way to measure your game than just score. If you know your stats, you can set realistic expectations. Setting realistic expectations can have a profound impact on your emotions and your reactions to shots.

It is not possible to influence score directly. Instead, your score is the sum value of how well you drive, approach, pitch and putt. If you hit more fairways and greens and have fewer putts, your scores will go down. Improve the parts to improve the whole.

There are all kinds of smart phone apps that do all the work of keeping stats for you. There really is no excuse not to track some aspects of your performance. Stats will help you make better strategy decisions, pick the right club and shot more often, and add more confidence to your swing. You'll know when to be conservative and when you can be aggressive.

Stats will also help you organize your practice and prioritize activities. Noting how many times you scrambled to get up and down would help prioritize which areas of your short game to prioritize. Was it chips, pitches, or lobs? Contact, direction or distance? Technique or skill? Trajectory or spin? The best time to identify which parts of your game need attention is right after you play. You'll also know how to address them with much greater clarity.

We have observed more and more golfers keeping notes on their phone, particularly juniors on the tournament circuit or college track. Journals are simple yet highly effective coaching tools. They will improve your self-awareness as well as provide insights into trends that lead to better game management and strategy decisions.

Coach's Advice

1. Be resilient. You're not going to win 'em all, so have a plan and a process to deal with it.
2. Play mentally tough. Use your emotions, rather than let them use you.
3. Have a pre-shot routine, a post-shot routine, and an in-between routine. They each accomplish different objectives and involve different skills, but they'll all help you get back to the present moment and balance your mind.
4. Cultivate a positive attitude toward pressure. The choice is yours. Make pressure your friend.
5. Even if the situation doesn't work out for you, if you've made a clear decision based on solid reasons, walk away with your head up. You'll get it next time.

Chapter 11: Clutch Action Steps

The only way to become a clutch player is through action. Get out there, face the challenges, and learn what it takes to prevail. The best way to succeed rapidly is to prepare in advance with the right kind of training.

In this chapter you encounter very detailed descriptions of Jeff Brehaut's preparation activities. Drawing from lessons learned over a 20-year career on the PGA Tour, he creates an endless variety of scenarios and challenges as he coaches the next generation of players.

His goal is to teach them more than just the swing. He's also teaching them how to think. He teaches them to recognize all the potential options, and how to best stack the odds in their favor. It's a structured process, yet there's plenty of room for creativity. He encourages experimentation and expects failures, but the focus is always on the lessons learned.

As you read through the coaching examples and scenarios, imagine creating the same situations and challenges for yourself. It makes practice a lot of fun, and sure beats pounding away at drivers all session.

Jeff Brehaut's Philosophy of Preparation

Jeff Brehaut played two decades on the PGA and Champions Tours. He won the grueling six-round PGA qualifying school in 2002, considered by many to be the toughest tournament in golf. Known as an elite ball striker, Brehaut was ranked No. 1 in Total Driving on the PGA Tour in 2004. He won the Callaway Invitational at Pebble Beach and notched multiple victories on the Nike Tour. Brehaut attended the University of the Pacific, where he played for Dr. Albaugh, and was inducted into the Pacific Hall of Fame in 2006.

Brehaut is now using two decades of PGA Tour experience to coach the next generation of young golfers. His stable of talented players are learning how to prepare through performance training, situational practice, and mindset. Brehaut's learned his philosophy of preparation the hard way:

> *"I've been on the good and the bad side of clutch situations many times, from junior golf to college golf to qualifying for the PGA Tour," said Brehaut in his clutch interview. "We were at Q-school at PGA West. I was confident and I was having a great round. I got to the last hole, and if I par the last hole, I was going to get my card. I hit a three-iron and pulled it in the water. That wasn't very clutch."*

But learning from past experiences is the key to doing better the next time. Brehaut discovered that the key for him was preparation, particularly spending more time practicing the situations he expected to face in the tournament. Preparation provided the foundation for success in clutch situations.

At the next Q-school, Brehaut was on the bubble once again. This time he faced a clutch putt: an eight-footer on the last hole to earn his Tour card. But he had prepared for that situation, staying late after his rounds to work on his putting, challenging himself to not go home until he made 20 putts in a row:

> *"The times when you're hanging around the number is when you find out what you've really got," said Brehaut. "When I got to that last putt to get my Tour card, I said to myself, 'Hey, I just did 20 in a row last night. This is just one more. Go ahead and knock it in.' And I did."*

Brehaut used positive self-talk to remind himself that he's done it before, and that he knows how to do it now. It's a powerful source of trust.

> *"I remember being on the first tee at the U.S. Open. There were tons of people watching and I was super nervous. Statistically my driver was my best club in the bag: I was number one in total driving the year before. But there I am, standing on the tee, and I'm afraid," recalled Brehaut. He had to step back and have a little chat with himself. "I remember thinking, 'You're better at this than everybody on the Tour. What are you so afraid of? Just go hit your shot.'"*

Brehaut's driving stats were a source of trust. Knowing he had earned trust in his driver kept him relaxed and focused. Brehaut hit his first drive in the center of the fairway, then went on to finish that day tied for the first round lead at Bethpage Black.

> *"Any experience you can draw on that gets you more focused and more trusting is going to help you be more relaxed and more confident. You draw on all those experiences, take a deep breath, trust yourself, and just go do it."*

When Brehaut transitioned into coaching juniors, he brought his philosophy of preparation with him.

He takes students on the course and puts them in real world situations they are likely to see on the course. He'll put them in the rough, behind a tree, or at an angle that brings a hazard into play. He recreates a clutch situation, then assesses their response.

> *"I put the ball in a so-so lie in the rough, 60 yards from the green, with a bunker in front. I said, 'You've got a two-shot lead, this is the last hole, what are you going to do?' And the kid dumped it right in the bunker. 'You'd better not do that in the tournament next week,'" I told him. "'Let's hit the ball 20 feet past the hole where all the green is.'"*

On-course coaching is an opportunity to assess all aspects of execution, from physical swing technique to strategy to mental focus.

Brehaut creates situations, evaluates the results, and then discusses alternative strategies and shots with his players. They may drop a few more balls in the same spot, try different clubs to vary trajectory and shape, and learn which strategies work best. Or they'll create different scenarios: *The pin's on the left side of the green, there's water to the left, and you're tied for the lead on the last hole.*

Brehaut wants his students to think in terms of improving the odds. He wants them to recognize, for example, when it is safer to be right of the hole, or even on a line to it, but also when it is too costly to be left of the hole. He assesses their ability to challenge their creativity in coming up with novel shots:

> *"Get a kid into a situation that he will eventually have to deal with, and see how he does," said Brehaut. "If they are right of the hole, they have a chance. Worst case they'll probably be in a playoff. But if they go left they are in the water and they lose the tournament. Then they can use that experience to make better decisions during competition."*

From these on-course assessments he creates training scenarios, using different situational shots on the range to practice for novel situations on the course.

> *"I'm giving a kid a scenario, picking a shot, deciding where the trouble is, where it's not, and having them perform," said Brehaut. "That makes it more game time."*

On the range he'll set up scenarios for training: "*There's two trees out at the end of the range. That's your fairway. Picture the holes that may give you trouble in the next tournament, fit them into the two trees, and see how many you can keep in the fairway.*"

The sky's the limit when it comes to imagining scenarios and shots on the range.

> *"It's like when we were kids practicing with our buddies," said Brehaut. "We'd be hitting putts around the practice green, and we'd say, 'This one is for the Masters' or 'This one is for the U.S. Open.' We were having fun, but we were also preparing for the biggest moments we could imagine. Now they're doing the same thing, but they're focusing more on situations they could face when they get to the big tournaments."*

The approach Brehaut uses to coach his juniors follows a proven process:

- Continually assesses students' capabilities in a wide variety of scenarios

- Plan range sessions and on-course lessons to address skill gaps
- Train for skills and shots they'll see in competition, using situational practice for different looks and shots
- Practice executing on the course, under the eyes of the coach, in novel and challenging situations
- Evaluate results by reviewing technique, strategy, and focus, and devise alternative shots and strategies where needed

The process engages students in a continuous looping cycle of improvement. Following a consistent process enables Brehaut to fast-track them to higher levels of performance.

Three Clutch Action Steps

Brehaut's students are learning to be clutch by developing the ability to think clearly in novel situations, trust their skills, and execute with confidence. These lessons came up time and again from high level players, which enabled us to identify three action steps common to virtually all clutch players, regardless of their sport:

1. Choose a *Can Do* mindset
2. Train at the edge
3. Do what works

We encourage you to start taking these three clutch action steps as soon as possible. Today would be fine.

Action Step 1: Choose a Can Do Mindset

Clutch is a mindset. Clutch players believe they can do it. And attitude is one of the few things over which you have total control. If you decide you are going to have a clutch mindset, you will. As Henry Ford said, "*Whether you think you can or think you can't ... you're right.*"

Clutch players have a clutch attitude. They maintain it by cultivating the intangible traits of high performers: confidence, resilience, adaptability, goal focus, present-centeredness, total task focus, and a selective memory.

Clutch players don't see setbacks as failures, but as opportunities to learn and improve. It is a mastery approach, where the emphasis is on continually seeking higher levels of play. It is a quest to see how good they can be. They embrace the challenge of the moment, viewing the turmoil arising from pressure as facilitative rather than counter-productive.

They view the moments when they put it all on the line as exhilarating, not debilitating. After all, as Sport Psychologist Matt Cuccaro said:

> *"The reason why we play isn't to be all calm, cool and collected. If that's the way we want to be, we'd be better off sitting at home on the couch."*

Hitting clutch shots is contagious. The more you do it, the more it happens, and the more it happens, the more confident you are that you can do it again. That confidence gives clutch players a certain sense of swagger. Clutch players aren't afraid to be bold. Jaime Diaz said in Golf Digest:

> *"There is a style and manner apart from results that is clutch. The athlete who possesses the poise and body language that clearly indicates he is 'embracing the moment' as today's sports psychologists urge, and who can also react to failure as a growth opportunity rather than a confidence crusher, will likely have what it takes under pressure."*

Clutch players know they can get it done. Muhammad Ali said, "*It's not bragging if you can back it up.*"

Adopt a clutch mindset. The decision is yours.

Action Step 2: Train at the Edge

Second, clutch players train for clutch situations. They're difficult shots at the edge of our capabilities, so they push the envelope. But with effort and expert guidance, the boundaries can be expanded.

High performance does not take exceptional talent, but it does take exceptional commitment. In Anders Ericsson's book *Peak,* he highlights a common misconception regarding what it takes to be a consistently superior performer:

> *"It is interesting to note that the vast majority of expert performers were not child prodigies; instead they were those willing to commit to organized practice regimens under the guidance of master teachers."*

The training done by high performers is not willy-nilly. They don't get better simply by putting in more hours. They get better by training the right things, the right way. Deliberately and with purpose.

Ericsson coined the term "deliberate practice" in the 1990s. The concept was later popularized in Malcolm Gladwell's *Outliers*, and has been shortened to the notion that it takes 10,000 hours of practice to reach expert-level performance.

But Ericsson's study points out that it is not 10,000 hours of any kind of practice. It takes deliberate practice, which he defined as:

> *"Effortful, structured learning that requires purposeful refinement and adaptation based on interpreting feedback for the specific intention of improving."*

Clutch players engage in structured, specific, deliberate training. They get detailed feedback. They make purposeful adjustments. They improve skills intentionally. They focus on improving results. They consciously train for tough situations.

Scott McCarron, for instance, is highly purposeful in his training. He never wastes a shot:

> *"I'm always moving targets, moving shots, hitting different shapes, doing the nine-ball challenge, playing holes."*

Clutch practice is working on the edges of your capability zone. It's stretching. It's attempting a wide variety of challenging but do-able shots. It's incorporating pressure in practice. It's training until execution is automatic because, as Jeff Wise notes in "Extreme Fear":

> *"Very well-learned skills seem to thrive under intense pressure. It's no coincidence that world records are often set at the Olympics, where the competition is fiercest and the stakes are highest."*

Changing your range time to train the right way isn't working. It's an investment you make in yourself that benefits your game. Training deliberately for clutch situations maximizes your ability to execute in any situation.

Action Step 3: Do What Works

Performing under pressure can only be learned through experience. Only by experiencing pivotal situations will you learn how you respond, and through that, which skills and techniques help most. The more opportunities you have, the sooner you learn to succeed. You have to go out there and do it. Tiger Woods said it in *Why I'm Clutch:*

> *"I've put myself there, in that situation, more times than anybody else. I've also failed more times than anybody else. But along the way, you do succeed."*

In order for that to happen, you first have to develop enough game to get into positions where you *can* hit crucial shots. For some golfers – especially new golfers – that may mean investing significant time on swing fundamentals to develop basic ball-striking skills. Solid swing fundamentals are vital. They are the foundation for taking your skills to the maximum of your abilities.

But once you can keep the ball in play, you'll discover that virtually every round of golf will present you with clutch situations. The first time you are about to break 100 will be just as nerve-wracking to you as trying to win a tournament is for a Tour rookie. When there's pressure to accomplish a goal, there will be clutch situations.

Catalog Your Observations

The secret to performing better in the clutch is to learn to recognize pressure situations, observe how you react, and then choose the response that will be most effective. Observe how you think, how your body reacts, and how your emotions change. With enough observations over time, you will discover your tendencies.

Pay attention as well to distracting thoughts that cause you to lose focus. Be aware of negative emotions that cause you to lose confidence and trust.

But also pay attention to what *works*.

Make special note of techniques that help you focus, control your thoughts, and manage your emotions. Rather than trying to fix what isn't working, build from your strengths. Focus on improving productive techniques and behaviors. Then find ways to integrate those techniques into your routine and execute them automatically.

You can't control the onset of negative emotions. They happen too fast and come without warning. But you can control the intensity, direction, and duration. Experiment with techniques to determine which ones help you regain control of focus, intention and trust, and then add them to your routine. Learn to execute regardless of emotional turmoil. The only way to really know what works is to get out there and do it when it counts.

Make the decision to be clutch. Then organize your practice sessions to deliberately learn and improve your performance skills. A confident mindset will emerge from those sessions. Apply all your skills when you play. Keep a record of how you responded in clutch situations to continually develop your skills through deliberate practice.

As We Practice So Shall We Play

All the clutch players we know prepare for clutch situations in their practice sessions. Make the effort to conduct quality practice sessions. The more efficient and effective you can make your practice sessions, the sooner you'll see results on the course.

Practicing realistic scenario shots under pressure will prepare you to make the shots when it counts. Practice resilience at the same time by bouncing back from mishits and errors.

Structuring competition on the range is an effective way to gain practical experience under pressure. Whether it is competing with another golfer or yourself – put something on the line. Make it matter. Be emotionally invested in the outcome so you feel some urgency. Competitions on the range are more than fun. They are a safe way to learn from failure. The more often you face the pressure of competition on the range, the more you'll thrive on the course.

Challenge your shot-making execution with drills that simulate on-course play. One club, one target, one shot. Full routine. No repeats. When mistakes happen, you learn to move on to the next shot, the same way you have to play it on the course. Simulated play is an opportunity to work on execution skills, and to identify tools and techniques that lift your performance.

Eventually you will find a variety of techniques that work for you. Once you've identified them, create a process around them so you know what steps to take and how to implement them on the course.

Practice the way you'll play.

Coach's Advice

1. Organize your practice time. Break it down by game areas and activities to make it as productive as possible. Be disciplined in your use of time.

2. Include Clutch Training. Every practice should have some component that simulates on-course play. Go through your entire routine. Select a different club and target for each shot. Make it as real as possible. Even better, include a reason to care. Imagine there is something on the line and that there are consequences. The emotional component simulates competitive playing conditions.

3. Practice Your Pre-Shot Routine. Set aside specific practice time in the beginning to develop a solid routine. Practice it until you can execute automatically. Then use your routine on every shot on the range and on the course.

4. Be resilient. When you fail (as you will), embrace it as a learning opportunity. Bounce back and resolve to get even better. Savor progress. Celebrate successes.

5. Practice adaptability. Different lies, yardages, conditions and situations require different adjustments. Adaptable swings give you more options on the course. Your process, however, remains consistent and become the anchor for execution.

6. Practice for contingencies. Know in advance how you will handle tough situations.

7. Keep a journal to record your observations about the way you play and practice. Review the journal periodically, and particularly at the end of the year, to help with planning for the next year. More and more golfers use their phone to store their journal notes.

8. Be clutch. Adopt a clutch mindset. Seek pivotal moments and a chance to excel under pressure.

****

APPENDIX: RESOURCES

Free Template & Downloads

Thank you for picking up the Clutch Golfer Formula. It is our sincerest hope that inside these pages you will find information that will help you have a lot more fun playing better golf. Helping golfers is our mission, and whether it is through books, videos, or on the lesson tee, our greatest reward is when students experience that "Aha!" moment that changes everything for them.

We have a number of companion templates and downloads that accompany the book. We encourage you to use them to get the most out of everything you have read. They are available free of charge.

Once you register, you'll have access to a variety of resources, including the Clutch Formula Template, a summary of the Coach's Advice from every chapter, and the Exercises compiled into a downloadable pdf. As we add more supplements and resources, they will automatically be available to you. Click or paste into your browser: https://igolfu.com/course/clutch-resources

Clutch Formula TEMPLATE

Step 1: Review the words below. Circle four words at each step that represent the highest priority skills or techniques to include in your routine.

LOCK	LOAD	FIRE	HOLD
• Analyze situation	• Action Cue (word, phrase or action):	• Remain focused	• Hold finish
• Pick specific target	• *Stay in rhythm*	• Stay committed	• *Suspend judgment*
• *Imagine shot shape*	• Set Up to ball	• Retain the target	• Acceptance
• Visualize trajectory	• *Take precise aim*	• *Swing in rhythm*	• *Feel Impact*
• Select Strategy	• Center mind	• Maintain trust	• Rehearse
• Pick club	• Center body	• Execute	• *4r's to Refocus*
• Narrow Focus	• Athletically ready	• Finish tall	• Positive self-talk
• Be intentional	• Focus	• Finish in balance	• Describe shot
• *Commit*	• Intention	• *Feel the swing*	• *Anchor*
• *Rehearse Feel*	• *Retain image*	• *Align body and mind*	• Adjusting swing
• Target Location	• Commit	• Free release	• Reinforcing swing
• Breathe	• Positive self-talk	• *Tension-Free*	• Finish
• Visualize	• *In sync*	• Release to target	• *Flow*
• Use Positive Self Talk	• Posture	• Connected	• Free
• Affirmations	• Center		
• Present-centered	• Breathe		
	• Waggle		

MORE FREE RESOURCES

The Clutch Test

We also have two more resources that are definitely worth checking out. The first is the Clutch Test. It's a free assessment of your skills at the four clutch pillars: Deliberate Practice, Focus, Intention, and Trust. It's fun and insightful. Take the test, and then pass the link along to your golfing buddies.

https://igolfu.com/clutchtest

CLUTCH TEST

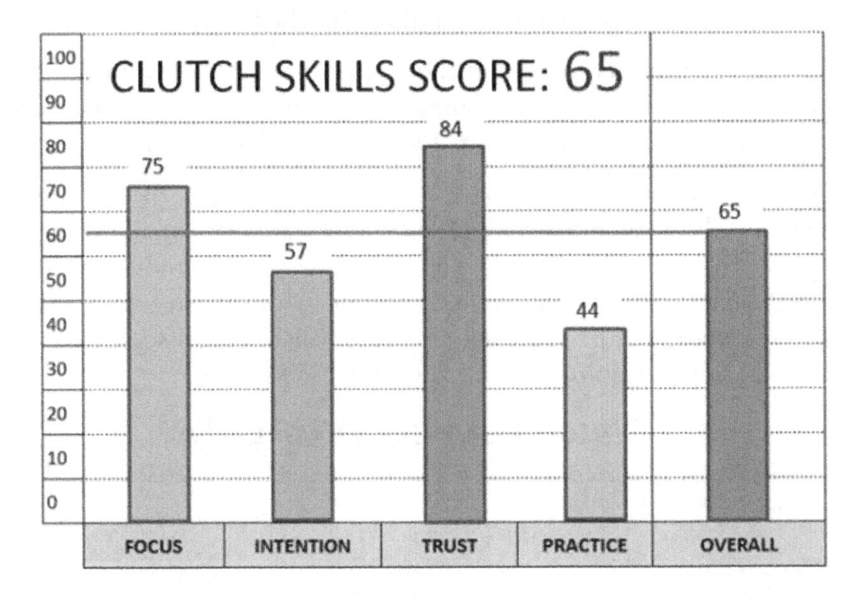

The Clutch Interviews

Second is the not-to-be-missed Clutch Interviews. They are insightful and inspiring 15-minute conversations with superstar players, coaches, and thought leaders. Also free.

https://igolfu.com/course/clutch-golfer-formula-podcast-interviews

****

Acknowledgements

Tour Players, Coaches, Luminaries

We give special thanks to the athletes, coaches and luminaries who contributed such fabulous stories for their Clutch Interviews. Their insights are priceless, and add depth and color to the fabric of the game: Jeff Brehaut, Pete Carroll, Bobby Clampett, John Dunning, Juli Inkster, Brandt Jobe, Scott McCarron, Nancy McDaniel, Michael Murphy, Conrad Ray, Kevin Sutherland, Kirk Triplett, Charlie Wi, Jeff Wilson.

CLUTCH GOLFER FORMULA PODCAST INTERVIEWS

Alpha Readers

Our hat is off to the intrepid golfers, our alpha readers, who provided their initial feedback on the book. We are eternally grateful for your time and energy and the constructive comments you provided on the initial draft: Allen Albaugh, Leith Anderson, Dick Barry, Beth Brown, Lisa Cobler, Sean Corte-Real, Miguel Delgado, Mike Dowd, Steve Falzone, Herbert Forster, David Harnden, Sharon Hornecker, Diana Kimbrough, Troy Kimbrough, Barbara Kraus, Brad Marek, Phil Marrone, Maureen Mcinaney, Kris Moe, Emmy Moore-Minister, Jim Nylen, Topper Owen, Fritz Poole, Barry Robins, Kevin Sverduk, Gabby Tapper, Jim Toal, Jeff Tokanaga, Hilton Tudhope.

Crowdsourced Editing

One of the most interesting aspects of writing this book was the editing process. Before hiring a professional editor, we used a process called "crowdsourcing" to get the book in its final form. Crowdsourcing involves inviting many people to contribute their thoughts to a project real time. We do it online, thanks to the ever-evolving advances in online technology, namely Google Drive and Google Docs. These tools allow multi-user access to an underlying shared file, with commenting and editing capability, as well as file version control. Crowdsourcing allowed us to tap into the collective wisdom of many golfers, leading to a final version that is far better than what any one of us could produce individually.

It was a fascinating experience.

Golfers are an amazing bunch. Maybe it's because no matter where we are we all share the same experience. We go into battle. We come out the other side. Along the way our triumphs and disasters create the stories that make up the warp and woof of the game we love. It's why we play, and it's that shared fabric of experience that makes golfers want to help other golfers.

Crowdsourced editing is not for the faint of heart. Many sections we thought were good had to be torn apart and rebuilt. It can be a humbling experience. Plus there were thousands of comments. Time-consuming as it was, we read and responded to every comment.

Crowdsourcing is an insightful, interesting, challenging, and ultimately rewarding experience. There is no doubt the book is better because of the insights of the contributors. You can understand, then, why we are deeply grateful to the golfers who volunteered to collaborate. We hope they got as much out of the process as we did.

Here are the golfers who took the time to crowdsource and collaborate with us to produce the final version of this book: Peter Adamo, Carlos Afonso, Quetzalaca Aguirre, John Allen, Brian Archibald, Andy Atkins, Michel Bachand, Brent Barker, Blair Barnett, Larry Baryshnik, Mark Bennett, Scott Benson, Thomas Bernthal, Joshua Bielke, Jim Bisch, Harvey Bishop, Robert Brady, Dennis Briley, Doug Cakebread, Tim Carroll, David Carruthers, Richard Coffey, David Collett, Rob Cote, Robert Daly, David Davies, Bob Dills, Ko Dooms, John Dranschak, Steve Ellison, Dino Ferrer, James Fleming, David Keen Fowler, John Freeman, Lyle Goodman, Ray Graham, Mark Grottoli, John Halligan, Steven Hansen, Joseph

Healey, Ryuko Hirota, Gavin Hudd, David Hughes, Jim Hussey, Jaz Jablonski, Lateef Jimoh, Sandor Juhasz, Kevin Kerley, John Lamb, Karen Larkin, Paul Larsen, Yun Lei, Orson Leong, Roland Loeve, Jim Loustalot, Jeff Marchant, Patrick Marichal, Ronald Mastroberti PGA, Adam Matthews, Jason Moffat, Daniel Monroe, Jakki Moxon, Chris Nail, Ron Nevin, Joanne Normandin, Peter O'Reilly, John Overman, Alan Parr, Peter Paul Paterno, Radim Pavlicek, Marc Philippe, Harold Pohoresky, Bob Pothier, Duane Raha, David Reed, Peter Rigsbee, Diana Rugg, Stephane Rugoni, Raju Samayam, Ernest Schmeisser, Jon Schram, Shel Schumaker, Chander Shenoy, Jeff Shilling, Raj Singh, Michael Singsen, Vivek Sood, Greg Tom, Daniel Tseng, Barry Turner, Peter Voss, Mark Walker, Carter Warren, George Watts, Steven Wonderlich, Brandon Xie, Chuck Yaeger, Byron Yep, Philip Young, Griff Whalen, Sarah Whalen, Scott Zimmerman.

Photo Credits

Cover: Jeff Brehaut holes out, courtesy Jeff Brehaut
Kirk Triplett trophy, courtesy Kirk Triplett
Kirk Triplett victory, courtesy Kirk Triplett
Guys in Green celebrate, USA Today
19th hole scene, Club Corp
Hammer, Hicaa.org
Juli Inkster at 2017 Solheim Cup, courtesy Juli Inkster
Scott McCarron, courtesy Scott McCarron
Pete Carroll Super Bowl, Pacific.edu by David Gonzales
Camera Lens, Unsplash
Bobby Clampett with trophy, courtesy Bobby Clampett
Eyeglasses, Unsplash
Trapeze artists, Unsplash
Driving Range, WikiCommons
Kevin Sutherland with trophy, courtesy Kevin Sutherland
Brandt Jobe with trophy, courtesy Brand Jobe
Stanford Golf 2019 NCAA Champs, courtesy StanfordPhoto.com
John Dunning, courtesy John Dunning
Pete Carroll, courtesy Alex Wood
Jeff Brehaut at Bethpage, courtesy Jeff Brehaut

About The Authors

Dr. Glen Albaugh

As one of the preeminent consultants in the field of Applied Sport Psychology, Dr. Glen Albaugh has coached the practical application of optimal sports performance to thousands of athletes and coaches of all levels. His college and high school clients have won state, national, and NCAA championships, while his PGA, LPGA and Champions Tour clients have won more than 50 events, amassing more than 70 million in winnings.

Dr. Albaugh has been a lifelong champion of inner game performance skills. His development of athlete-centric self-coaching models in the 1970s, along with work by contemporaries including Bob Rotella, Bruce Olgivey, Keith Henchen, Ken Ravizza, and Rich Gordon, played an influential role in the development of the Association for Applied Sport Psychology.

In 1989 Dr. Albaugh traveled to Russia, with Legendary Hall of Fame 49ers coach Bill Walsh and Michael Murphy of the Esalen Institute, to study Soviet Olympic athlete training and coaching programs. Those meetings influenced the direction of American performance-based coaching paradigms from the Olympics to professional sports to colleges, high schools and youth coaching. Nearly every player on Tour today has a mental skills coach on their support team with roots tracing back to Dr. Glen.

Dr. Albaugh is Professor Emeritus at the University of the Pacific. He received his Ph.D. from the University of Utah in 1970, and then joined the Pacific faculty, where he taught for 28 years. Former students include Hall of Fame football coach Bill Walsh, and Pete Carroll, Seattle Seahawks head coach. Dr. Albaugh was also the Pacific Men's Golf Team head coach for 16 years, leading them to 15 NCAA Championship appearances. He was inducted into the Pacific Hall of Fame in 1983, and received the coveted Pacific Mentor Award in 2016.

An international keynote speaker, Dr. Albaugh has conducted numerous workshops for the PGA, LPGA, and Nationwide Tours, as well as the PGA of America and the National College Coaches Association. He was awarded honorary lifetime membership in the Northern California PGA in 2016.

In 2006, Dr. Albaugh collaborated with Michael Bowker to write Winning The Battle Within, a bestselling comprehensive book for Golf Performance Psychology. Winning The Battle Within features performance practice, managing thoughts and emotions, and self-coaching strategies for peak performance. The book is a journey into the inner game, where all great performances arise. Dr. Albaugh was inducted into the California Golf Writers Association Hall of Fame in 2014.

Visit Dr. Albaugh's website www.wbwgolf.com, where you can order your own copy of his landmark book *Winning the Battle Within: The perfect Swing is the One You Trust.*

Eric Jones

Eric Jones is an award winning PGA Class "A" teaching professional. He was named 2014 PGA Teacher of the Year in Northern California, and in 2016 was recipient of the NCPGA Horton Smith Award for Education Excellence. He is a graduate of Stanford University and holds a Masters Degree in Sport Psychology from John F. Kennedy University.

Eric is a former assistant Coach at Stanford University, where he also played his college golf. In 2003 he captured his first World Long Drive Championship title, and followed with his second world championship title in 2012. He was named the LDA Tour Rookie of the Year in 2004. Eric is the creator of The 5 Keys to Distance, the longest-running and most popular distance training program in golf.

In addition to operating several teaching academies in Northern California, Eric is the author of numerous golf instruction books, including several best-sellers: *Play Strategic Golf: Course Navigation*, and *How To Make A Yardage Guide*, both available on Amazon. He is a frequent Keynote Speaker, has presented educational seminars for the PGA, and is an Advisory Board member for several golf industry companies. He is a member of the Board of Directors of the JGANC (Junior Golf Association of Northern California), the oldest junior tournament organization in Northern California.

Eric is the founder of iGolfU.com, where he is leading the evolution of online golf instruction, performance training, and coaching.

Thank You

Thank you for investing your time and attention to finish this book. Our coaching has always been focused on finding the best and most effective ways for golfers of all abilities to play to their peak performance capabilities. We hope this book has given you the tools and approach you need to succeed.

We leave you with this quote from legendary basketball hall-of-famer Michael Jordan: *"Some people want it to happen, some wish it would happen, others make it happen."*

It's time to get out there and make some clutch happen

NOTES

Made in the USA
Monee, IL
31 July 2020